AFO
MASSIMILIANO AFIERO

AXIS FORCES 2

WW2 AXIS FORCES

The Axis Forces 002 - First edition April 2017 by Soldiershop.com.
Cover & Art Design by soldiershop factory.   ISBN code: 978-88-93272407
First published by Soldiershop, copyright © 2017 Soldiershop (BG) ITALY.   No part of this publication may be reproduced, stored in a retrieval system or transmitted by any form or by any means, electronic, recording or otherwise without the prior permission in writing from the publishers. The publisher remains to disposition of the possible having right for all the doubtful sources images or not identifies. Visit www.soldiershop.com to read more about all our books and to buy them.

In merito alla specifica serie Italia storia ebook serie Ritterkreuz l'editore Soldiershop informa che non essendone l'autore ne il primo editore del materiale pervenuto dall'associazione Ritterkreuz, declina ogni responsabilità in merito al suo contenuto di testi e/o immagini e la sua correttezza. A tal proposito segnaliamo che la pubblicazione Ritterkreuz tratta esclusivamente argomenti a carattere storico-militare e non intende esaltare alcun tipo di ideologia politica presente o del passato cosi come non intende esaltare alcun tipo di regime politico del secolo precedente ed alcuna forma di razzismo.

Note editoriali dell'edizione cartacea

Copyright per l'edizione cartacea italiana della Associazione Culturale Ritterkreuz di Via San Giorgio 11, 80021 Afragola (NA). La riproduzione delle foto qui pubblicate è severamente vietata Il primo editore ha compiuto tutti gli sforzi necessari per contattare i titolari dei diritti di alcune delle illustrazioni riprodotte, e si impegna a riparare a eventuali errori o omissioni nelle future edizioni del presente testo.

The Axis Forces

in World War Two 1939-1945

The Axis Forces number 2 – Avril 2017

Direction and editing
Via San Giorgio, 11 – 80021 AFRAGOLA (NA) -ITALY

Managing and Chief Editor: Massimiliano Afiero

Email: maxafiero@libero.it

Website: www.maxafiero.it

Contributors

Stefano Canavassi, Carlos Caballero Jurado, Rene Chavez, Antonio Guerra, John B. Köser, Lars Larsen, Christophe Leguérandais, Erik Norling, Scott Revell, Raphael Riccio, Marc Rikmenspoel, Johannes Scharf, Charles Trang, Cesare Veronesi, Sergio Volpe

Editorial

Here we are finally with the second issue of our new magazine. We would like to remind everyone that for the time being our publication will appear on a quarterly basis which means that our next issue, barring any unforeseen problems, will appear in early July 2017. We would like to take the opportunity to thank of our readers who have been a part of this new editorial adventure and to thank all of our many and ever increasing number of contributors who, from around the world, are lending a hand to further our project of military historical research relating to Axis formations of the Second World War. In this issue, I hope that you will find the articles and subjects to be of interest, and as always we invite you to suggest new subjects that you would like to see covered in forthcoming issues. Warm greetings to everyone and so long until the next issue.

Massimiliano Afiero

The publication of The Axis Forces deals exclusively with subjects of a historical military nature and is not intended to promote any type of political ideology either present or past, as it also does not seek to exalt any type of political regime of the past century or any form of racism.

Contents

The Flemish Legion	Pag. 5
Felix Steiner and the European Volunteers	Pag. 26
The Wiking and the battles in the Izyum area, July 1943	Pag. 34
SS-Unterscharführer Max Rudolf Pesarra	Pag. 41
The Italian SS Legion	Pag. 46
Foreign Volunteer Legion Military Award & Insignia	Pag. 53

The Editor hereby declares that every effort has been made to trace the owner's right of the photographic material published on this issue. Unfortunately every search and query has been unsuccessful. If and whenever the proprietor(s) of the these rights would contact us producing documentation testifying such rights the Editor will recognise the appropriate fee.

The Flemish Legion
by Antonio Guerra

SS-Standartenführer **Michael Lippert.**

The Flemish Legion parading in Brussels.

In early July 1941, a Flemish legion was created that at first was named *Verband Flandern*, then *Landesverband Flandern*, then *Bataillon Flandern*, and finally *Freiwilligen–Legion Flandern*, intended for combat duty on the Eastern Front. For a certain period of time the legion and *SS-Regiment 'Nordwest'* had to coexist, and even until the end of August there were 850 Flemings within the regiment. The *Nordwest* was finally disbanded on 24 September 1941 and its Danish, Dutch and Flemish soldiers were then transferred to their respective national legions. The three companies that had Flemish volunteers were consolidated, forming the *SS-Freiwilligen Verband Flandern*, subordinate to the *SS-Ostubaf.* Michael Lippert. At the same time, a heavy weapons company and a reserve company were formed. At the end of July, the first contingent of Flemish volunteers was transferred to the Debica training camp to complete its military preparations. The campaign to recruit volunteers was sponsored by the principal Flemish nationalist parties. The exception was Staf de Clerq, head of the *V.N.V.*, who at least initially did not support the recruitment campaign. At all of the recruiting centers throughout Flanders a total of 1,200 volunteers joined up, most of whom came from the nationalist movements, but after the stringent medical exams conducted by the meticulous German doctors, only 405 of them were accepted into the Legion.

Formation and training

In order to officially sanction the creation of the Legion, on 6 August 1941, a great ceremony was organized in Brussels; the reviewing stand was draped with large banners exalting the brotherhood between the Flemish and German peoples, and paying tribute to the fight against Bolshevism, while the 405 volunteers of the Legion along with an honor guard from the

Nordwest regiment stood in front of the reviewing stand. Immediately following the ceremony the new volunteers were accompanied to the railway station, applauded by a crowd of civilians, loaded aboard the train, and transferred to the training grounds at Debica in Poland, where they joined the rest of the *Nordwest* Regiment and the Dutch volunteers of the Dutch Legion; supervising the training was the commander of the *Nordwest*, *SS-Standartenführer* Otto Reich. The Flemish volunteers adapted with difficulty to the harsh training program imposed by the German instructors; discipline was iron, and the official language, as well as the training personnel, were German. In fact, aside from the patch with the lion of Flanders sewn on the left shoulder, there was nothing else Flemish in the Legion!

SS-Staf. Otto Reich.

Flemish volunteers training, autumn 1941.

Waffen-SS volunteers training with an *MG-34*.

Most days for the new recruits began at five in the morning and ended late in the evening; much time was dedicated to sports activities, in the perfect style of *Waffen SS* training. Selectees for specialist training (engineers, artillerymen, communications specialists, etc.) were sent to various training schools; a group of Flemish volunteers was sent to Breslau to the Engineer School, while another group was sent to the Signals School in Nuremberg. The entire 4th Company was transferred to Hamburg for specialized training with heavy weapons. In an attempt to try to resolve problems of "settling in" of the volunteers, Staf de Clerq requested and was granted a meeting with Himmler. The *Reichsführer-SS* tried to resolve the delicate situation, increasing the number of Flemish officers and NCOs in the unit and guaranteeing the equivalency of ranks between the Belgian Army and the legion. Finally, he ordered the German personnel to learn Flemish culture and customs, in order to be able to behave better with their "students".

Staf de Clerq reviewing volunteers of the *Zwarte Brigade*.

Flemish volunteers training, 1941.

Flemish volunteers training, Autumn 1941.

Flemish volunteers during an official ceremony, 1941.

In August 1941, several hundred of the students, including Reimond Tollenaere, the former deputy and head of the *Zwarte Brigade* of the *VNV*, joined the Legion. Along with him were Jef François, of the Flemish Militant Order, Paul Suys, of *Rex-Flanders*, the Flemish branch of the movement headed by Degrelle, and René Lagrou, head of the Germanic SS in Flanders. Along with other former officers of the Belgian Army, they were all awarded the rank of *SS-Unterstrmführer*. During that period the Legion, still under command of *SS-Ostubaf.* Michael Lippert, was directly subordinate to the *SS-FHA*.

Transfer to East Prussia

On 3 September 1941, the Flemish volunteers were transferred to the camp at Arys in East Prussia for the final phase of their training. There, a few days later, another

150 new volunteers arrived, coming from the *13.* and *14. Kompanie* of the disbanded *Nordwest* Regiment, and which formed the *5. Kompanie* of the Legion consisting of two anti-tank platoons and one mortar platoon. The Dutch volunteer Legion was also transferred to the camp at Arys to continue joint training with the *Flandern*, also under command of *SS-Standartenführer* Otto Reich. On 24 September 1941, the order arrived from SS headquarters in Berlin for the unit's official designation, which had become a reinforced motorized infantry battalion: the *SS-Freiwilligen Legion Flandern*. The Flemish unit was thus elevated to SS status.

Flemish volunteers training with an *MG-34*, Autumn 1941.

General Berger inspects the Legion.

The Flemish volunteers were allowed to wear the twin-rune SS insignia, although many of the troops coming from the former *Nordwest* preferred to wear the *Trifos* as a badge of distinction on their uniform. The *SS-Freiwilligen Legion Flandern* was organized as a reinforced infantry battalion with five motorized companies with a total strength of 1,112 men: (25 officers (of whom 14 were Flemish), 78 NCOs (one of whom Flemish), and 1,009 soldiers (935 Flemish). On 13 October 1941, the Flemish volunteers swore an oath to Adolf Hitler, as supreme commander of the German armed forces, but as established by the agreement, "...only in the fight against Bolshevism". In the spring of 1941, the order of battle of the Flemish Legion was as follows:

The Axis Forces

Flemish volunteers being instructed in the use of *Mauser KAR 98K* rifles, Autumn 1941.

Training with a Mortar, Autumn 1941.

Commander: *SS-Ostubaf.* Michael Lippert
Adjutant: *SS-Ustuf.* Günther Steffen
Aide: *SS-Stubaf.* Urbain Bohez
Logistics Officer (Ib): *SS-Ostuf.* René van Eyndhoven
Intelligence Officer (Ic): *SS-Ostuf.* Albert Seipold
Medical Officer (IVb): *SS-Ostuf.* Adalbert Dr Prix
Medical Assistant: *SS-Ostuf.* Dr. Michel
Dentist (IVd): *SS-Ustuf.* Herbert Hepburn
Stabs-Kompanie: *SS-Ustuf.* Steffen, 103 men
1.Schützen Kompanie: *SS-Ostuf.* Peter Nussbaum, 220 men
2.Schützen Kompanie: *SS-Ustuf.* Helmut Breymann, 218 men
3.Schützen Kompanie: *SS-Ustuf.* Hans Moyen, 219 men
4.(Schwere) Kompanie: *SS-Ustuf.* Karl Neuhäuser, 223 men
5.(Pak) Kompanie: *SS-Ustuf.* Karl Weingärtner, 159 men

The three rifle companies consisted of three rifle platoons and a heavy weapons platoon. Each heavy weapons platoon had two heavy machine guns plus a section of light mortars. The 4th "heavy weapons" company consisted of three platoons of heavy machine guns and a heavy mortar platoon. The 5th anti-tank company had two Pak platoons, each equipped with three 37 mm anti-tank guns and a heavy mortar platoon.

On 27 October 1941, the unit was inspected by *SS-Brigdf.* Kurt Knoblauch, chief of staff of *Kommandostab Reichsführer-SS*, who soon after reported to Himmler that the Flemish legion was ready for employment at the front. On 6 November 1941, the unit received its orders for transfer to the Eastern Front, in the Leningrad area, more specifically, in the Tossno sector. The Flemish Legion was to be subordinate to *the 2.SS-Infanterie.Brigade*, commanded by *SS-Brigadeführer* Gottfried Klingemann.

The Eastern Front

Flandern operational area, between 1941 and 1942.

On 10 November 1941, the Flemish volunteers left the Arys training area in four motorized groups; they covered 180 miles on the first day and the Legion bivouacked in the area of Kreuzingen, near Tilsit. On 13 November, the leading elements of the unit penetrated into Soviet territory and reached Pskov. The following day, the Legion reached Rozhdestwjenno, marching through an area that was infested with partisans; the *Feldgendarmerie* had set up numerous checkpoints and at each one had to provide explanations and march orders because no one was aware of the arrival of this new unit of foreign volunteers on the Leningrad front. After having passed through Tosno along the Leningrad-Moscow railway line, on 17 November 1941, the Legion's staff reported to the headquarters of *2.SS-Inf.Brigade* at Chudovo near Tarasovo (Tarasowa). The Flemish volunteers suffered severely from the difficult weather conditions of the Eastern Front, characterized by polar temperatures.

SS-Brigdf. Klingemann.

An SS soldier escorting a partisan captured in the rear area.

The *1.Kp.* and *2.Kp.*occupied Andrijanowo, *3.Kp.* in a nearby hamlet, while *4.Kp.*, *5.Kp.* and the Legion staff were billeted in Tarasovo. The arrival of the Flemish Legion significantly strengthened the *2.SS-Inf.Brigade*. In addition to the *Flandern*, at that time the SS Brigade also included two battalions of *SS-Ing.Rgt.4*, and the *SS-Begleit–Bataillon 'RF-SS'* under the command of *SS-Hstuf.* Massell, the *SS-Flakabteilung Ost* commanded by *SS-Ostubaf.* Karl Burk, and other minor units. At that time the SS Brigade comprised the mobile reserve of

XXVII.Armee-Korps within the framework of the great German offensive against Leningrad and its units were employed mainly in the rear areas against partisan bands.

Sleigh of the *2.SS-Infanterie-Brigade* (*Charles Trang Collection*).

A Flemish legionnaire, 1941.

First actions

On 24 November 1941, the first Flemish *Kampfgruppe* consisting of a platoon from each of the companies of the Legion, commanded by *SS-Ostuf.* Peter Nussbaum, was engaged in combat. Flemish *SS-Ustuf.* Reimond Tollenaere, Jef François and Paul Suys were part of the detachment. At 0700 on 24 November, the *Kompanie Nussbaum* moved towards the front lines, taking up positions at Pogostije, Maluska, Bawatski and Olumno. Most of its sub-units were placed under command of the *SS-Begleit –Bataillon 'RF-SS'*. The Flemish volunteers then moved to the area south of Tossno (Rublejewo), to provide protection for the railway line that linked the cities of Mga and Kirishi south of the Maulska swamps. Positioned immediately behind the front lines, the Flemings found themselves fighting at the same time against both Red Army units and against partisan bands that roamed the rear areas. On 3 December 1941, *Kompanie Nussbaum* was relieved by another Flemish company, commanded by *SS-Ustuf.* Breymann; this included most of *2.Kompanie*, and part of *3.Kompanie*. The replacements took over the positions that had been occupied by the *Kompanie Nussbaum*. That same day a reconnaissance patrol led by *SS-Ustuf*. Hans Mojen was sent out to reconnoiter the dense forest in front of the Flemish positions.

A German defensive position with a *Pak*, December 1941 (*Hubert Kuberski Collection*).

A Soviet partisan unit during an attack, December 1941.

After having advanced into an area that was totally infested by partisan forces, the patrol fell into an ambush and was almost completely wiped out; at least six Flemish volunteers were killed, and another three were seriously wounded. On 4 December, several Soviet patrols attacked a column of *Wehrmacht* vehicles west of Olomno in an attempt to seize the supplies being transported. Units of the *SS-Begleit –Bataillon 'RF-SS'* as well as a company from *Flandern* then joined the action, pushing the enemy units back and inflicting heavy losses. The Flemings suffered only three wounded. On 6 December, the *Heeres-Panzerjäger-Abteilung 563* replaced the Flemish volunteers in the area of Tarasovo and the *2.SS-Inf.Brigade* handed over its positons to the *250.Inf.Div.*, the *Division Azul* (the Spanish Blue Division), consisting of Spanish volunteers, with the Flemings going to a rest area in Latvia. The *Flandern* Legion followed and was transferred to its winter quarters between Sabile and Kandava.

A German defensive position on Leningrad front, December 1941.

Soldiers of the *Division Azul*.

An *MG-34* machine gun on heavy tripod, December 1941.

A Russian gun fires at German positions, December 1941.

Also on 6 December, Flemish legionnaire Frans Coulombier was awarded the Iron Cross Second Class for having distinguished himself in defensive combat operations on 27 November 1941, during an attack carried out by partisan forces at Pyendikovo. This was the first ever German decoration awarded to the Flemish Legion.

The Soviet response

On 9 December 1941, in the context of the surprise Soviet winter counteroffensive, enemy forces retook the position at Tikhvin, throwing the German forces to the other side of the Volchov River. With the arrival of the winter season and the sudden decrease in temperature, combat operations were scaled back drastically; the front lines thus became a series of strongpoints, where individual units fought in isolation, struggling mainly against hunger and the cold. All of the motor vehicles froze up, as did automatic weapons. In order to overcome the cold, the soldiers resorted to drinking brandy, rendering them continuously drunk and subject to attacks of dysentery. Beginning on 18 December, units of the *2.SS-Inf.Brigade* began to displace to Latvia, in the area between Tuckum and Pleskau. The Flemish units also reached Latvia, in the area of Ape, beginning on 20 December. Until 31 December the companies were located as follows: staff and headquarters company in the sanatorium at Sabile, *1.Kp.* at Sabile and *2.*, *3.* and *5.Kp.* at Kandava, while *4.Kp.* was billeted at a large farm near Sabile.

A German infantry unit on march, December 1941.

An SS sentry sheltering from the cold.

A German defensive position on Leningrad front.

On 1 January 1942, the commander of the *2.SS-Inf.Brigade*, *SS-Brigdf.* Klingemann, called a conference of all units subordinate to him to discuss the military situation; the Soviets were attacking along the entire Eastern Front and it was necessary to send units immediately to the front line to strengthen the defenses on the Leningrad and Volchov fronts. Two days later, *SS-Ostubaf.* Lippert formed a *Kampfgruppe*, under the command of *SS-Ustuf.* Breymann, consisting of *2.Kp* and *4.Kp.*, with a total of 7 officers, 24 NCOs, 312 soldiers and about 40 trucks. *Kampfguppe Breymann* was attached to the *SS-Begleit –Bataillon 'RF-SS'*. The Flemish *Kampfgruppe* gathered together at Sabile on 9 January 1941. From there, aboard trucks, the volunteers were transferred to Volmar, covering 220 kilometers over nightmarish roads.

A *PzKpfw.III* with infantry aboard, in the Tikhvin sector.

A German infantry unit on march, January 1942.

Soviet infantry attacking the Flemish positions.

Waffen-SS riflemen returning enemy fire.

On 10 January, the Flemings reached Torma in Estonia and on 12 January, after having crossed the Narwa River, reached Kingisepp. In the meantime, the temperature had fallen to less than forty degrees below zero Celsius. On 17 January, the *Kampfgruppe* reached the sector of Podbjerjezhje-Iwanovskoje.

The battle for Koptsy

The Soviet forces had succeeded in penetrating the German defensive line in many points and the situation appeared critical: *4.Kp./Flandern* had taken up positions at Tyerymeyts, a few hundred meters from Podbjerjezhje, alongside Spanish units of the Blue Division. On 18 January, *Kampfgruppe Breymann* received orders to prepare for an attack scheduled for the following day; the village of Koptsy and the road and section of railway line that passed through that sector had to be retaken. A tank from a German army unit was to support the attack. *SS-Ustuf.* Breymann planned the attack along with his platoon leaders; the three infantry platoons of *2.Kp./Flandern* were to make a frontal attack, while the heavy weapons of *4.Zug* of *Ustuf.* De Wilde were to provide supporting fire. At dawn on 19 January, German artillery began firing. Soviet artillery quickly responded to the fire; the Flemish volunteers attacked, in spite of the deep snow and the exchange of artillery fire. When the fire began to become more intense, the volunteers halted, seeking shelter where they could. *SS-Ustuf.* Breymann had to intervene personally to convince his men to resume the attack. The advance of *3.Zug* on the left side of the road proceeded more quickly because it was not hampered by Soviet artillery fire.

Soviet artillery on the Leningrad front, January 1942.

A German assault group with an *MG-34*, January 1942.

A destroyed Soviet *KV-1* and German soldiers, January 1942.

Once they had arrived on the outskirts of Koptsy the riflemen of the first platoon threw themselves against the enemy positions; the Soviets quickly opened fire with all of their weapons, inflicting numerous losses. *Uscha.* Sohelleder was among the first to fall to the enemy fire, but this did not stop the Flemish assault. The assault forces led by *Uscha.* Ritzau and Sauer of the third platoon worked strenuously to to try to distract the enemy fire directed against the first platoon of *SS-Ustuf.* Vieweger and the second platoon under *Ustuf.* Tollenaere. The action was successful and the two platoons were able to resume the assault against the Soviet trench line. Opening the way, hurling a number of hand grenades, the Flemings managed to get the upper hand. In the furious close-quarters combat that followed, the Soviets were thrown from their positions and forced to fall back towards the center of the village. Meanwhile north of Koptsy a *Wehrmacht* reconnaissance unit had seized the main road, eliminating any possibility of escape by the Soviets. After having eliminated the last pockets of resistance, the village fell into Flemish hands. Several Soviet units deployed further to the east began to hit the village with fire from rocket launcher batteries.

A German defensive position on the Leningrad front, January 1942.

Ustuf. Reimond Tollenaere.

At dawn on 20 January, after having hit the village with their artillery, the Soviets attacked Koptsy in force, quickly making their way into the center of the village. The Flemings reacted quickly, unleashing furious hand-to-hand combat; around the command post of the 2nd Company, which was in an old partially destroyed house; the fiercest fighting took place in a veritable tangle of men compressed into a few square meters of space. *Ustuf.* Reimond Tollenaere came out of the house like a devil, armed with a light machine gun firing rapid bursts which he used to cut down all of the Soviet soldiers he encountered. Thanks to the supporting fire from the heavy weapons of *Ustuf.* De Wilde, the Soviets were finally forced to withdraw after suffering heavy casualties. *SS-Ustuf.* Vieweger received orders to lead a patrol along the Koptsy-Zapolye road to follow the enemy's movements.

SS-Obersturmführer **Helmut Breymann.**

An *MG-34* firing against the enemy, February 1942.

Once the situation had stabilized, the Flemings were able to work on consolidating their positions and strengthening their defensive posture. Breymann, having in the meantime been promoted to the rank of *SS-Obersturmführer*, set up his command post close to that of the 4th Company in Zapolye on the eastern bank of the Volchov River; the two Flemish companies thus found themselves defending along a five kilometer front that ran from the western suburbs of Koptsy to Nowaya Bystritsa to the east of the Volchov River. On 21 January, the first supplies arrived from the army depot at Podbjerjezhje. The next day, 22 January, *Ustuf.* Tollenaere and de Wilde made an inspection tour of the Flemish positions; during the inspection, Soviet artillery heavily shelled the entire front and *Ustuf.* Reimond Tollenaere was killed as a result of an exploding shell.

Gruppe Debes

On 30 January 1942 the elements of the Legion that were still in Latvia reached Kampfgruppe Breymann at Podbjerjezhje. Only a few minor units such as the repair platoon remained at Sabile. The *Flandern*, the *SS-Flak-Abt 'Ost'*, and the *SS-Begleit-Bataillon 'RFSS'* were thus left to form the *Gruppe Debes*, under command of *SS-Obf.* Lothar Debes. On 1 February 1942, *SS-Ostubaf.* Lippert reported to Debes at Lyublyady to receive orders; the Flemings were subordinated to *Infanterie-Regiment* 424 of the 126.*Infanterie-Division*, commanded by *Oberst* Harry Hoppe. The units of the legion established defensive positions between Koptsy, Zwemtitsy, Zapolje, Andrjuchinowo, Twutitsy and Krutik, where they were engaged in heavy combat. The second and fourth companies subsequently passed under control of the *Inf.Rgt 422* commanded by *Oberst* von der Golz. The *Flandern* command post was set up at Andrikhnovo along with most of the 3rd Company. On 4 February, the second and fourth companies, after having been heavily engaged in defensive combat and having sustained heavy casualties, were transferred to Podbjerjezhje for a short period of rest.

Flemish volunteers during an official ceremony, February 1942.

A group of Flemish volunteers, February 1942.

On 10 February 1942, units of *Flandern* were again cited in the German war bulletin:"...*During defensive operations against massive enemy attacks the 25th Motorized Infantry Division of the Wurttemberg and the SS Flemish Legion distinguished themselves particularly*". From 13 January to 19 February 1942, the *126.Inf.Division* and units attached to it repulsed fully 109 enemy attacks launched by 28 regiments belonging to about a dozen different Soviet divisions. On 14 February, the last of the units arrived from Latvia: the 1st Company of *SS-Ostuf.* Nussbaum, with a strength of 2 officers, 13 NCOs, and 117 men was assigned to a defensive position between the villages of Bolshoye and Zamozhye. At the same time the 2nd and 3rd companies were transferred to the Zwemtitsy sector, about three kilometers northwest of Koptsy. The next day, 15 February, the Flemish units were engaged in beating back fresh enemy attacks. Support from *Stukas* was necessary to stem the massive attacks, especially those that were being supported by armored forces. On 16 February, the command post of the *SS-Begleit –Bataillon 'RF-SS'* suffered direct hits from the Soviet artillery and most of its officers, among them the battalion commander, *SS-Stubaf.* Grimme, were killed. *SS-Stubaf.* Lippert thus assumed command of the *SS-Begleit –Bataillon 'RF-SS'* as well as of the *Flandern* Legion.

Flemish volunteers manning a mortar, February 1942.

A soviet machine gun in German service.

During that period the Legion was reinforced by the following units:

- 9.Kp. Genesenungs-Rgt.647
- 2.Kp. Landesschützen –Rgt.232
- Kradsch.-Zug/ SS-Begleit –Bataillon 'RF-SS'
- Nachr.-Staffel/ SS-Begleit –Bataillon 'RF-SS'
- Flak-Zug/Regiment 'Hoppe'

The companies of the Legion were repositioned to the left of the Wjeshki-Zwemtitsy road, northwest of Andrjuchinowo. Effective strength had fallen to 12 officers, 41 NCOs, and 335 soldiers, for a total of

388 men. Despite the fact that the units were exhausted, they had to remain on the front line and had to launch a counterattack in the Zyemptitsy sector.

Sturmmann Emiel Mertens.

Flemish volunteers of *3.Kompanie/Flandern*, March 1942.

A member of *Nordwest* Rgt. Assigned to *Flandern*.

The conquest of Zyemptitsy

Beginning on 2 March 1942, the Flemish units were engaged along the Vyeshki-Zyemptitsy road in a counterattack to halt a Soviet penetration. Two assault groups had prepared for the action. The first group, commanded by *SS-Ostuf.* Nussbaum, consisted of the 1st Company with several machine guns and mortars from the 4th Company. The second group, under the command of *SS-Ustuf.* Eckenbrecher, consisted of the 3rd Company and other heavy weapons from the 4th Company. The remainder of the 4th Company was held in reserve while the 5th Anti-Tank Company took up positions behind the two groups. The 37 mm guns of the *RFSS* reserve battalion were about 400 meters to the rear. After preparatory artillery fire the Flemings went on the attack. Leading the attack were the squads commanded by *Oberscharführer* Fritsch and Jensen of the 1st Company. Unfortunately Fritsch's squad and *Ostuf.* Nussbaum ended up in a minefield and the detonation of several mines resulted in several dead and wounded.

The crew of an infantry support gun belonging to *Flandern*.

A Flemish volunteer defending a trench, march 1942.

A German defensive position on the Leningrad front, 1942.

A cry quickly went out for medical personnel to the front line to attend to the numerous dead and wounded. The advance of the other units also made little progress; subjected to a heavy crossfire from the enemy weapons, the Flemings were stalled for three hours. In an attempt to give fresh impetus to the attack, *SS-Ostubaf.* Lippert sent *SS-Ustuf.* Weingärtner with additional troops to the positions where the Flemish troops had been stopped by the enemy fire. At the same time, *Uscha.* Völki, commander of a heavy machine gun platoon of the Nussbaum Group's 4th Company, reached the right flank of the Soviet positions and began to take them under fire with his heavy weapons. Thanks to the providential fire support the Flemings were able to push forward, occupying the most forward of the Soviet positions and several bunkers.

While the Nussbaum Group had been stalled, the second assault group had managed to overwhelm the Soviet positions on the left; the Flemish engineers destroyed the remaining enemy bunkers that continued to resist with explosive charges. Further to the northwest a battalion of the Spanish Blue Division advanced to protect the exposed flank of *Flandern*. For the rest of the day the Flemings methodically combed the area to eliminate the last packets of enemy resistance. Towards nightfall all of the objectives had been reached but losses were heavy: the Legion had suffered the loss of two officers, nine NCOs, and 110 men including dead and wounded.

A Flemish volunteer. Note the Legion sleeve patch and cuff title.

Among the fallen was *SS-Ostuf.* Nussbaum; after being seriously wounded by an exploding mine; he died while being transported to a hospital. *SS-Ustuf.* Weingärtner had been quite seriously wounded by a piece of shrapnel from an exploding mine.

The attack resumed the following day, 3 March 1942; *SS-Untersturmführer* Wieweger led the assault of what remained of the first and third companies and of a heavy machine gun platoon. The few survivors of the 2nd Company were assigned to another combat group under command of *Oberscharführer* Rüter. The Wieweger assault group had to cross a large snow-covered field under the covering fire of the heavy weapons of the 4th Company's heavy machine gun platoon. Rüter's men had to march along the right side of the field, parallel to it. Several Spanish units of the Blue Division also took part in the attack. *Kampfgruppe Rüter* was the first unit to advance upon the Soviet positions, engaging in hand-to-hand fighting and capturing four enemy bunkers. Before attacking the Soviet positions, Vieweger's men took measures to establish contact with the Spanish battalion commanded by *Major* Roman.

Spanish volunteers of the *Division Azul*, March 1942.

A German *MG-34* in position.

A Flemish patrol advancing in enemy territory.

After a short pause, to avoid the enemy's artillery fire, Flemings and Spaniards attacked shoulder-to-shoulder. The Soviets did not waste any time and brought all of their weapons to bear against the mass of advancing enemy soldiers. After having advanced about three hundred meters, Vieweger's men had to halt and take shelter from the fire of the Soviet machine guns and mortars, as did the Spaniards as well. Around nightfall the volunteers dug trenches and foxholes in the snow in order to gain some protection against the cold and the enemy fire. The next morning, the Flemings launched a fresh attack and were able to eliminate the enemy's forward positions. During the assault, *Flandern* lost *SS-Ustuf.* De Wilde, commander of the 5th Company, and 19 men killed or wounded. On 5 March, a battalion of *Inf.Rgt.422* relieved units of the Legion which were then transferred northwest of Zyemptitsy. During the transfer march, Soviet artillery harassed the withdrawing Flemings, claiming additional victims.

Sturmmann Remi Bogaert.

During the same day, *Ustuf.* Rene van der Smissen, a native of Hansbeke, was killed in combat at Weschki. On 6 March, there were long-range engagements between the artillery and heavy weapons. The Soviet positions were about 250 meters from the Flemish positions. During the morning, elements of the Legion were once again assembled for a new offensive action. A new assault group was formed consisting of the second and third companies of *Flandern* and a German reserve company. An anti-tank gun from the 5th Company was in support. The first, fourth and fifth companies formed a second assault group that was deployed along the main road to Zyemptitsy. This group was soon after reinforced with part of the 2.*Kompanie*, some elements of *Inf.Rgt.422*, and two anti-tank guns. The new attack against Zyemptitsy began at eight o'clock in the morning, after half an hour of preliminary shelling by German artillery. Advancing under enemy fire, the Flemings pushed forward for about 200 meters until they were close to the enemy positions. Overhead the *Stuka* dive bombers supported the infantry attack by bombing the enemy trenches. Firing and throwing grenades, the Flemish volunteers and German soldiers leaped into the enemy positions, occupying them after bitter close-quarter combat. Around noontime, the first combat group managed to penetrate the southern part of Zyemptitsy and ten minutes later the second group entered the northern part of town. For several hours reconnaissance patrols combed through the area to eliminate the last pockets of Soviet resistance. Around 1700, the two Flemish combat groups sent a brief message to the *Flandern* headquarters: "...*Zyemptitsy in our hands. Ivan Kaputt!*". Four hours later, *II./Inf.Rgt.422* arrived to relieve the Flemish units from the position. The toll in losses for *Flandern* was however heavy: two NCOs and five legionnaires dead, *Ustuf.* Mojen, five NCOs and eleven legionnaires wounded, and three legionnaires lost (captured by the Soviets). On 8 March, at 2200, the Legion, whose effective strength had fallen to barely 108 men fit for duty, was pulled from the front line and placed in reserve under *XXVII.Armee-Korps* at Chichulino, near Novgorod.

Bibliography

M. Afiero, "*The 27th Waffen SS Volunteer Grenadier Division Langemarck: an illustrated history*", Schiffer Publishing, Atglen 2016.

M. Afiero, "*27.SS-Freiwilligen-Grenadier-Division 'Langemarck'*", Associazione Culturale Ritterkreuz, Ottobre 2014.

A. Brandt, "*The Last Knight of Flanders*", Schiffer Publishing Ltd.

R. Landwehr, "*Lions of Flanders*", Shelf Book

Felix Steiner and the European Volunteers
by Johannes Scharf

SS-Standartenführer Steiner in 1936.

Felix Steiner in Poland, September 1939.

In March 1914 Felix Martin Julius Steiner, born on May 23, 1896 in Stallupönen (East Prussia), his father being a teacher, joined the 5th East Prussian Infantry Regiment "von Boyen" No. 41 in Tilsit. Having joined as a cadet he was promoted to 2nd Lieutenant within less than a year of service after he had participated in the battles near Tannenberg, on the Masurian Lakes and in Lithuania. He had been severely wounded in autumn of the year he had joined but fortunately recovered very soon. On June 18, 1914, being a Lieutenant already as mentioned above, he received the Iron Cross 2nd Class and was transferred to a different unit where he was made company commander. After having fought with his men on the Courland front in 1916 and having participated in attacking and conquering Riga he was presented with the Iron Cross 1st Class. In the last part of the war he saw action in Belgium and France as well where he took part in the bloody matériel battles. It was there in fall 1918 where he received his promotion to 1st Lieutenant. Despite the fact that the war itself was over and his unit had been demobilized in Danzig the fighting wasn't over yet for Steiner and a lot of men of his kind. He knew that the struggle in the East had to continue for the sake of his German compatriots who where now all of a sudden no longer living on German territory. So in January 1919 he was again found to be in the position of a company commander – but now he was leading a Free Corps unit in East Prussia. Incorporated into the *Reichswehr* in 1921 he then worked in different headquarters, participated in various inspection trips with the Generals' headquarters and by 1932 had become the training leader at West Land Police inspectorate before leaving the *Reichswehr* again in 1933. After he had been promoted to Captain in December 1927 he retired from the *Reichswehr* having attained the rank of *Major*. Felix Steiner who had joined the SA and was transferred to the SS in April 1935 very soon began to develop new training techniques and especially tactics which had nothing to do with the disastrous stationary warfare he and his men had seen in World War I. Together with Paul Hausser he laid the foundation of the *SS-Verfügungstruppe* which was the predecessor of the *Waffen-SS*. Whereas Paul Hausser was still somewhat clinging to the opinions of the old general staff Steiner was a completely new type of strategist, in many ways not unlike Heinz Guderian. In his concept for basic military training physical capability was very important and another focus lay on the soldiers' and officers' mutual trust. Another officer who had a very similar opinion on training techniques and tactics was Cassius Freiherr von Montigny with whom – among others – he established the indeed legendary *SS-Junkerschule* in Bad Tölz.

Steiner pass the *SS-Regiment 'Deutschland'* in review, Autumn 1940.

Awarding decorations.

Autumn 1941: *SS-Brigdf.* Steiner in Russia, with two officers of *Wiking*, Köller and von Schalburg (*Bussano*).

When World War II broke out he was leading the VT unit *SS-Standarte "Deutschland"* as *SS-Oberführer*. He had taken command of the unit in summer 1936 as *SS-Standartenführer*. He led his unit in all the upcoming campaigns: after having participated in the occupation of Czechoslovakia in 1938 this by the outbreak of the war meant the *blitzkrieg* in Poland in 1939 and the Battle of France in 1940 which also included the invasion of the Netherlands. His regiment had fought outstandingly wherever it had engaged the foe in combat. For the battles in France and the successful conquest of the Walcheren peninsula in the Low Countries Steiner was awarded the Knights Cross of the Iron Cross on August 15, 1940. Only a few months later, in December 1940, and after being promoted to the rank of *SS-Brigadeführer*, he assumed command and oversaw the shaping of the newly created *Waffen-SS-Division "Wiking"* which was a division made up of mostly non-German volunteers who came from countries like the Netherlands, Norway, Denmark, Finland, Sweden and Belgium.

L'*SS-Brigdf*. Steiner in Russia 1941, while discussing with other officers of the *Wiking* Division.

SS-Gruppenführer Steiner in Russia, Winter 1942.

Steiner with Finnish Volunteers.

Steiner with Danish volunteers, 1943.

But there were even volunteers from Switzerland in the ranks of the new unit which formed a brotherhood beyond borders and was so to speak the spearhead of the anti-Bolshevist youth. For the merits of the fine *Waffen-SS-Division "Wiking"* during Operation *Barbarossa*, Steiner was presented with the Oak Leaves to the Knight's Cross in December 1942. In April 1943, he was to become the commander of the *III.(Germ.)SS-Panzer-Korps* and for leading this unit outstandingly Felix Steiner – by then *SS-Gruppenführer* and Lieutenant General of the *Waffen-SS* – received the Swords to the Knight's Cross on August 10, 1944. Steiner's III (Germanic) Panzer Corps had played a major role in the defensive battles at Narva – and during the Battle of the Tannenberg Line, also known as the Battle of the European SS, withstood a great Soviet force with only seven tanks left. In the Battle of the Tanneberg Line 136,830 Soviet troops were held off by 22,250 men. Felix Steiner who by the end of the war had become an *SS-Obergruppenführer* and General of the *Waffen-SS* was released from incarceration in 1948. Before, at the Nuremberg Trials all charges against him had been dropped. 1958 he then published a book which was entitled *"Die Freiwilligen der Waffen-SS. Idee und Opfergang"* (The Volunteers of the Waffen-SS. Idea and Sacrifice) and discussed the foundations on which the European movement of volunteers had been built in its first chapters and documented the incredible achievements and examples of loyalty and camaraderie in its second part. The sacrifice of the European volunteers culminated in the defence of Kolberg by French soldiers and the defence of the Reichshauptstadt Berlin by Danes, Norwegians, Swedes, Latvians and again French volunteers.

Left, *SS-Gruf*. Steiner with *Ritterkreuz mit Eichenlaub*. Right, the commander of the *III.(Germ.)SS-Panzerkorps*, *SS-Ogruf*. Steiner presents the Knight's Cross Estonian *SS-Ostubf*. Harald Riipalu, 1944.

Hitler with Steiner and *SS-Stubaf*. Degrelle at award ceremony after the Battle of Cherkassy, February 1944.

As the Soviet troops advanced on Kolberg, the majority of its inhabitants as well as approximately 70,000 German refugees who had been trapped in the Kolberg Pocket were evacuated by the *Kriegsmarine* in the last days of the war. Also the remaining 40,000 German soldiers were evacuated from the besieged city and only around 2,000 soldiers were left to cover the last sea transport on March 17, 1945. Due to a lack of anti-tank weapons, the

German naval forces used the guns of their battleships to support the defenders of Kolberg. Yet I want to focus on the second part of Steiner's book in this article: Were the volunteers of the *Waffen-SS* a European avant-garde? The former commander of the so called "Vikings" in his afore mentioned book talks about a fundamental transformation of the men which occurred – regardless of what rank they may have held – after they had seen the horrors of Bolshevism and the suffering of the Ukrainian peasants with their own eyes.

Left, Steiner speaks with Norwegian Prime Minister Vidkun Quisling during the review of the Norwegian SS Legion in the Novgorod region, 1942. Right, Estonian volunteer, Harald Nugiseks.

Steiner and Derk Elsko Bruins.

While most of them had seen themselves as Dutch, Danish or Norwegian nationalists before this experience they now had become truly European idealists. They now indeed regarded themselves as knights of the west who fought a common enemy – just like in 1529 and 1683 when Vienna was twice saved by a combined European force from getting conquered and pillaged by the Turks. "*All of a sudden*", writes Steiner, "*the volunteer in vast Russia realized that Dutchmen, Danes, Norwegians and Germans here fought for their common native land. In his comrade next to him he perceived a person who had a similar way of life and the same historical background – and in view of the enormous masses of the foe realized the imperative of the common front.*" Disagreements which had i.e. existed in Belgium between Flemings and Walloons were now obsolete. And what *"had been forgotten in Europe in the one and a half centuries of separation now awoke in him [the volunteer] as overwhelming experience of war. In the midst of the fratricidal war of the European peoples the idea of a common European destiny was born on the frontlines against [...] Bolshevism, mentally comprehended and executed in the struggle."* While within the ranks of the Western Allies nationalism was still virulent and the masses of people without rights on the Soviet side were driven to more and more blood sacrifice by the thought of world revolution, the European idea had a wonderful renaissance *"in the hearts of the volunteers"*.

Latvian volunteers, Summer 1943. On the left, *SS-Stubaf.* Veiss.   Soldier from *'Handschar'*.

Dutch Volunteers in training, 1941.

A new breed of soldiers had been shaped which henceforth thought European. Steiner nevertheless stresses that in his opinion the European volunteers of World War II were just one link in a chain and he forges a bridge from Lützow's Free Corps over Lord Bryon's and Giuseppe Garibaldi's volunteers, Josef Pilsudski's Polish Legion and the volunteers of World War I to those who served in the *Waffen-SS*. Felix Steiner is annoyed about the ignorance of some higher-ups concerning the recruitment of Eastern Europeans at the outbreak of the war against the Soviet Union, for Estonia, Latvia and Western Ukraine had always regarded their heritage as European. *"According to their way of life and their historical development they were the frontier bastions of Europe"*, he writes. All essential preconditions for a very strong movement of volunteers if not for a people's uprising hat been met in the Baltic countries and perhaps less so in the western part of Ukraine. Instead of enforcing and strengthening the voluntary formations and self-protection units and incorporating them into the *Wehrmacht* as companions in arms they were in fact disarmed very soon due to orders of the German civil administration. In spite of that there was an incredible number of Estonians, Latvians and Western Ukrainians who at a time when the Soviets were regaining lost ground and the Germans were in peril joined the ranks of the *Waffen-SS* and tried to stop the red flood.

Reichsführer-SS **Himmler inspects soldiers of** *14.Waffen-Grenadier-Division der SS*, **1944.**

French volunteers at Sennheim camp, 1943.

They all shared the hardships of their German comrades until the bitter end without hesitation. In steadfast loyalty they stood their ground regardless of their nationality: Scandinavians, Belgians, French, Swiss, Spaniards, Italians, Latvians, Estonians and many more. They didn't break their oath and fought in order to liberate Eastern Europe from the evils of Bolshevism and to protect those countries which had not yet fallen into the hands of the Soviets from the red plague. The awareness of European solidarity had awoken in their hearts and minds, the awareness also of the fact that *"the characteristic achievements of European culture had come into existence through collaboration of the European peoples and stemmed from a common root."*

SS-Ogruf. **Steiner with Danish Volunteers.**

To the contrary the youth of every country had been raised in the belief that the history, literature and art of their particular people was a whole – a thing complete in itself – and not the result *"and a part of a greater intellectual unity."*

In the preface of *Die Freiwilligen*, Felix Steiner expressed the hope that now (1958) the public opinion had perhaps shifted and the heat of the debate which had been dominated by post-war propaganda had somewhat cooled down so people could carefully look at the facts presented in the book and come to an own opinion. Unfortunately at the beginning of the 21st century we must state that however vox populi hasn't only stayed the same as immediately after the war but has changed a lot to the worse indeed. Following generations haven't come to their senses and it seems like the – sometimes ridiculous – lies which were and are inflicted upon the new generations by school teachers, politicians and Hollywood film directors regarding the brave men of the *Waffen-SS* and the German soldiers who fought in World War II in general have in fact made them that way.

Norwegian Volunteers of *Den Norske Legion* on the Eastern Front, Winter 1941-42.

Who will speak up for the brave volunteers once the last of them will have been consigned to the grave? Lest we forget their sacrifice! *"If all become unfaithful, we remain loyal / So that there will always be a Fähnlein for you on earth."*

The Wiking and the battles in the Izyum area, July 1943
By Marc Rikmenspoel

The situation in Summer 1943 on the Eastern Front.

Narwa Panzergrenadiers, **Summer 1943.**

The Soviet plan for defeating the German Kursk offensive involved launching counteroffensives north and south of the main battle zone. The Soviets usually disguised their intentions with Maskirovka techniques, but in this case, they openly carried out preparations to attack the German Orel salient, to the north of Kursk, and the Donets and Mius River lines to the south. They correctly believed this would draw German armor reserves away from the Kursk area, and would keep those reserves dispersed. Wiking had ended the 1943 winter campaign in positions along the Donets, near Izyum. There, it reorganized and partially refitted during the lull from April through June. The division had suffered heavy casualties in the fighting since the advance to the Caucasus that began in late July, 1942. It was further weakened by giving up the Finnish Volunteer Battalion, whose contract was expiring, and the *Nordland* Regiment, which was becoming a cadre for the *III.(Germanisches) SS-Panzerkorps*. With *Nordland* went many officers and NCOs from other elements of *Wiking*, along with hundreds of Germanic volunteers. Some of the latter also had expiring service contracts, others were joining the in-formation *Nederland*, *Langemarck*, and *Wallonien* Brigades. The third battalion of *Germania* had left *Wiking* temporarily, to reequip as a SPW (armored halftrack) battalion. In return, *Wiking* received the first combat-ready battalion of the Estonian Legion. It was detached and retitled *SS-Panzergrenadier Bataillon Narwa*. The *Westland* Regiment had spent the preceding campaign organized as a two-battalion "light" regiment, but now reverted to a standard organization, with *Narwa* functioning as its third battalion. Limited personnel replacements also arrived, but *Wiking* was far from full strength as the summer of 1943 began, with only five infantry battalions and an understrength tank battalion. As such, it received a reserve role for the Kursk offensive, as part of the *XXIV.Panzerkorps*. In early July, it was moved north from the Izyum zone, to a staging area near Belgorod. *Wiking* was to be ready to reinforce the southern pincer of the German offensive, but the attack was halted before it could be committed.

XXIV.Panzerkorps commander Walther Nehring stands between *Wiking* Division commander Herbert Otto Gille and *I./Germania* commander Hans Dorr, shortly before the Izyum fighting.

On July 16, the Red Army showed signs that it was about to attack across the Donets. *Wiking* was alerted during the day, and started heading back to its former deployment area. Rainy weather turned the roads to mud and slowed *Wiking's* arrival. The anticipated offensive began on July 17, as the *46. Infanterie Division* was pushed out of its positions at Bol. Garashevka and Mal. Garashevka. If left uncontained, the offensive could have advanced to Barvenkovo, where it would have interdicted the main north-south rail line the Germans used for supplying units in the Stalino-Mius sector. However, simply by drawing *Wiking* away from the Kursk zone, the offensive had accomplished its primary purpose. *Wiking* began arriving in the Donets zone in the early hours of July 18. Hans Dorr and his *I./Germania* were the first unit to reach the area. The headquarters of the *XXXX.Panzerkorps*, responsible for the Donets front, demanded a quick assault, before the Soviet bridgehead across the river could be expanded. Dorr therefore prepared his men to assault through the village of Ssrednij, and then wheel to the west-northwest and roll up the Soviet positions by taking the two Garashevkas. The next battalion to arrive, Günther Sitter's *I./Westland*, would follow and support Dorr's attack. Dorr's attack began at daybreak. He led his men in storming through Ssrednij, but as they emerged from the west end of the village, they were stopped by extremely heavy Soviet fire from across the Donets. Soviet tanks emerged from Bol. Garashevka, to make the situation worse. Caught in the open, there was nowhere to seek cover and the battalion was nearly destroyed. Dorr gathered several machine gun squads, and with them drove Soviet forces off a nearby hill, which relieved some of the pressure.

Germania Regiment commander Jürgen Wagner has just received the Knight's Cross he was awarded on July 24. Gille, at right, used his own piece for the ceremony, which is why he isn't wearing it. Joining the celebration is *Westland* Regiment commander August Dieckmann. (*NARA*).

Dorr was wounded in the upper arm, and passed command of the remnants of his battalion to German Cross in Gold holder Walter Iden, the *1.Kompanie* commander. It was the eighth of sixteen wounds Dorr suffered during the war. Iden led the battalion south to the state farm (kholkoz), where it began to regroup. Sitter and the *I./Westland* followed *I./Germania*, as planned. They finished clearing Ssrednij, but then had to fend off repeated Soviet counterattacks. By the next day, the battalion was mostly surrounded, and defended itself in an all-around hedgehog fashion. The heavy weapons of *4.Kompanie* played an important part, especially the guns of the antitank platoon, which was led by Albert "Pak" Müller. The

4.*Kompanie* commander, German Cross in Gold holder Werner "Bubi" Gruben, was killed-in-action during the fighting on the 19th, and it is likely that Müller assumed acting command in place of him. The *I./Westland* was also nearly destroyed while defending Ssrednij through July 21. As Dorr and Sitter attacked Ssrednij on July 18, German Cross in Gold holder Hans Juchem and his *II./Germania* arrived at the kholkoz (to which Iden would later retreat).

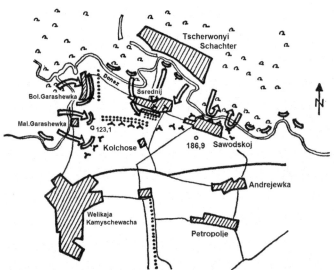

A map of the Izyum battlefield, taken from Peter Strassner's *European Volunteers*.

Heinz Juchem wears a shirt made from Heer camouflage material, as he speaks into a field telephone. This photo was probably taken during the summer 1942 advance towards the Caucasus.

Juchem could see Soviet attack forces pushing through Savodskoye, just east of Ssrednij, and moving to the high ground south of the village. He led his battalion in an attack which occupied the commanding Hill 186.9, and pushed the Soviets back towards Savodskoye. A few hours later, in the evening, after repulsing a counterattack against the hill, Juchem and his men stormed and occupied Savodskoye. They then moved south to screen and protect the village of Andrejevka, while German Cross in Gold holder Walter Schmidt and his *II./Westland* took over the defense of Savodskoye. At the same time, Georg Eberhardt and his *Panzergrenadier Bataillon Narwa* dug in on Hill 186.9. While Ssrednij remained under heavy attacks, the main Soviet effort seems to have been directed a bit to the east. Savodskoye itself was constantly attacked on the 19th-21st, but additional Soviet forces, led by tank brigades, bypassed the village on either side, trying to get over Hill 186.9 and make a clean breakthrough. Roughly a quarter of Narwa was on leave during this battle, leaving 650 men present. Nearly half of them would become casualties by the 21st. *Narwa* had three 50mm antitank guns, and three 76.2mm former-Soviet antitank guns. These took a terrible toll of the attacking tanks, while Estonian infantrymen used hollow charges to knock out several more. The worst fighting was on July 21, when Narwa began to run out of antitank and machinegun ammunition.

Georg Eberhardt was killed in action on this day, which infuriated his exhausted men, and spurred their continued will to resist. Another Soviet attack on Hill 186.9 might have successfully broken through, but the Red Army formations were temporarily out of tanks, after losing almost 100 on the hill and at Andrejevka. Juchem's adjutant, Heinz-Wolf Kölzig, personally knocked out two Soviet tanks that broke into Andrejevka on July 19.

A newspaper photo from the spring of 1943, showing Georg Eberhardt on the left. In the foreground is German Governor-General for Estonia Karl Siegmund Litzmann. He was making an inspection of the Estonian Legion at the Debica/Heidelager troop training grounds.

He did this by single-handedly operating a captured Soviet 76.2mm Ratsch-Bumm that was near the *II./Germania* headquarters (Narwa's ex-Soviet guns had been issued when the battalion arrived at the front, while the gun Kölzig used was captured on the 18th or 19th). Other tanks that got through the frontline positions of the Estonians and of Juchem's men were destroyed by the few long-barreled Panzer IVs of *3./SS-Panzer Abteilung 5*, which were led by Helmut Bauer. The rest of the battalion, with *Panzer III*s and *Sturmgeschütze*, fought in small groups all over the battlefield, aiding the defense where they could. The main Soviet attacks ended after July 21. Fighting continued, but the Soviet breakthrough to Barvenkovo had been denied. *Wiking* was battered, and needed over a week of rest to recover. As suggested above, dispersing and wearing down the German armored forces was the true goal of Soviet operations in the second half of July, 1943. This was achieved in this Donets battle, and it was even more successful to the south, on the Mius River, where the rest of the *XXIV.Panzerkorps* fought alongside the *SS-Panzerkorps*). The Soviet bridgehead there was destroyed, but the *Heer* and *Waffen-SS* Panzer Divisions that accomplished this suffered even more heavily than did Wiking, after most had incurred serious losses at Kursk. When these divisions, and *Wiking*, rushed to the key Belgorod-Kharkov area during August 1943, they were too weak to do more than delay the main Soviet offensive there. New Soviet offensives on the Donets and the Mius were then able to overrun the German infantry divisions left to defend those sectors. The Germans were soon retreating to the Dnieper River, and the initiative had passed to the Red Army for the remainder of the war. Wiking's commanders used the lull after July 21 to recommend their subordinates for high decorations. Germania commander Jürgen Wagner was awarded the Knight's Cross

Albert "Pak" Müller poses with his parents while on leave, after receiving his Knight's Cross.

already on July 24. Walter Schmidt, Albert Müller, and Georg Eberhardt all were awarded the Knight's Cross soon after, on August 4. Hans Juchem, Günther Sitter, and Helmut Bauer had to wait a bit longer, but had their Knight's Crosses approved on September 12. By that time, Juchem had become the second winner of the Close Combat Clasp in Gold in the entire German military, with his medal dated August 10.

Walter Schmidt seen circa May, 1944, after the Cherkassy fighting. He has removed the decorations from his pockets and his Knight's Cross, won for his battalion's defense of Savodskoye, has been slung unusually low. Schmidt won the Oakleaves to his Knight's Cross on May 14, 1944. This photo was likely taken in such a way that a press agency could add in the Oakleaves, above the Knight's Cross, and possibly other decorations, for an article announcing the high award. He hadn't been flown to Hitler's headquarters yet, for the customary personal presentation of the Oakleaves.

Günther Sitter has just received his Knight's Cross, circa the second half of September, 1943.

Helmut Bauer posed for this portrait after receiving his Knight's Cross. Note the "5" on his shoulder boards, in recognition of his serving in *SS-Panzer Regiment 5*.

He was killed in action three days later, and never knew of his Knight's Cross. Other men had their roles in the July, 1943, fighting recognized later, with subsequent battles also being part of their award criteria. Izyum provided one incident among several for numerous German Cross in Gold recommendations. In particular, Heinz-Wolf Kölzig won the award on December 7, 1944, with most of the cited combats occurring that year. Hans Dorr's Oakleaves to the Knight's Cross, awarded on November 13, 1943, reflected numerous combats from 1942 and 1943, with one of them being his actions outside Ssrednij. The battle *Wiking* waged along the Donets, during late July, 1943, deserves to be better-known. The division was pushed to the limit in the fighting. Its own counterattack failed, but it then successfully withstood three days of heavy Soviet assaults, which were well-supported by armor, artillery, and air power. Not for the first time, nor for the last, *Wiking* had scored a local victory in a campaign the Germans lost.

Bibliography

Jurs, August, et al. *Estonian Freedom Fighters in World War Two*. Canada: The Voitleja Relief Foundation Book Committee, n.d.

Klapdor, Ewald. *Viking Panzers: The German 5th SS Tank Regiment in the East in World War II*. Mechanicsburg, PA: Stackpole, 2011.

Regimentskameradschaft des ehemaligen SS-Panzergrenadier Regiments Nr. 10 "Westland." *Panzer-Grenadier der Panzerdivision "Wiking" im Bild*. 2d ed. Osnabrück: Munin, 1987.

Strassner, Peter. *European Volunteers*. Winnipeg: Fedorowicz, 1988.

Trang, Charles. *Wiking Volume 3*. Bayeux: Editions Heimdal, 2016.

Yerger, Mark C. with Ignacio Arrondo. *German Cross in Gold Holders of the SS and Police, Volume 7*. San Jose: Bender, 2014.

Yerger, Mark C. with Ignacio Arrondo. *German Cross in Gold Holders of the SS and Police, Volume 8*. San Jose: Bender, 2015.

SS-Unterscharführer Max Rudolf Pesarra
by John B. Köser

SS-Uscha. Max Rudolf Pesarra.

Max was born on the 16th February 1923 in Heidig. He joined the *Hitlerjugend* at fourteen on the 30.4.1937 and remained a member until 5.5.1941. After his schooling, Max work as a clerk for the forestry commission and volunteered for the *Waffen-SS* in January 1941. He was accepted and on 5th May 1941 was posted to *"Totenkopf"* being sent to *SS-Kaserne* Nürnberg to be trained as a telephone operator in *1./SS-Nachr.-E-Abt.Nürnberg*[(1)]. After one month's training, Max was transferred on 5.6.1941 to *Nachrichten Stab II./SS-TK.Inf.Rgt.1*. Max spent the next 13 months with this unit, which was attached, with the rest of the Division, to General Erich Hoepner's Forth Panzer Group under command of *Generalfeldmarschall* Wilhelm Ritter von Leeb's Army Group North. Leeb's force was tasked with advancing on Leningrad and formed the northern wing of Operation *Barbarossa*, but would have to wait in reserve during the initial phase of the invasion. Initially stationed at the Div. Staff staging area at Taplau. It was not until the 24th of June 1941 that the division would be used to mop up any enemy stragglers in the forest around Jurbarkas in Lithuania. Completing this by late afternoon on the 26th, *SS-Totenkopf-Division* received orders to advance to Deguciai but by this time the Russians had recovered from their initial paralysis and began to offer strong resistance. On the 28th June, *SS-Totenkopf-Inf.Rgt 1* repeatedly engaged wandering isolated groups of Russian soldiers, who fought to the death rather than surrender to the SS troops.

Summer 1941: advance into Russia.

Their actions could not be understood by the *Waffen-SS* troops and *SS-Standartenführer* Max Simon concluded that these groups of Russian soldiers must be armed "bandits" and consequently the majority of Russian stragglers were shot. The next day, the regiment was sent over the main vehicle bridge at Dünaberg to reinforce the division and was employed offensively, along the Dunskaja-Izvalta road to prepare for the later employment of the division in that direction. Fighting against weak enemy resistance the regiment reached the line Zidina-Lipinski later the same day at 17:30 hours.

Summer 1941: *SS-Totenkopf-Division* **in Kraslava.**

However the enemy was employed with stronger forces in the forests on both sides of the Zindina, Kraslawa and Lipinski roads and resistance intensified but by the 2nd July 1941 the division had captured Kraslava with the regiment eliminating or causing the enemy, two soviet infantry regiments along with tanks and artillery to retreat from the city. Continuing its advance into Russia the soldiers of the division had little time for rest and the fought hard for every small advance against a determined Soviet force. They finally captured Opochka by the 11th July 1941, after sixteen days of continuous combat, and managed a few short hours rest before continuing the push east. *SS-Totenkopf-Division* along with the rest of Army Group North continued its advance until it ground to a halt around Lake Ilmen in October 1941.

Max Pesarra in 1941, Eastern Front.

1941: interrogation of Russian peasant.

Autumn 1941: advance into Russia.

Soldiers of *SS-Totenkopf-Division* in Russia, 1941.

Award of EKII for these soldiers of *Totenkopf*.

As the Russian winter set in the division was incapable of further advancement having endured, as Eicke claimed, near a 50% casualty rate since the beginning of the invasion. Eicke's superiors denied his requests to remove the division from the front line, so they dug in and prepared to endured the Russian winter.

In the Demyansk pocket

Throughout the winter the Russians prepared a massive counter attack against the weakened German forces being designed to sever the link between the German Demyansk positions, and the Staraya Russa railway that formed the lines of communication of the German 16th Army. However, owing to the very difficult wooded and swampy terrain, and heavy snow cover, the initial advance by the Russians was very modest against stubborn German opposition. Therefore, on 8 January 1942, a new offensive called the Rzhev–Vyazma Strategic Offensive Operation was begun, which slammed into SS-TK's defences southeast of Lake Ilmen. At the same time the second phase of the northern pincer offensive began and by 20 May 1942, had successfully encircled the German 16th Army's and parts of the X Army Corps. Trapped in the pocket along with the troops from SS-TK were the 12th, 30th, 32nd, 123rd and 290th infantry divisions as well as RAD, Police, Organization Todt and other auxiliary units, for a total of about 90,000 German troops and around 10,000 auxiliaries.

Kirilowitschip (Max seated middle).

Machine gun position Demyansk, 1942.

EKII Damyansk 1942.

Hermann Göring had assured Hitler that the encircled troops could be supplied from the air using *Luftflotte 1* via the two viable airfields at Demyansk and Peski which were capable of receiving transport aircraft. From the middle of February 1942, the weather improved significantly, and while there was still considerable snow on the ground at this time, resupply operations were generally very successful due to inactivity of the Soviet airforce in the area. However the operation did use up all of Luftflotte 1's transport capability, as well as elements of its bomber force. Over the winter and spring, the Northwestern Front launched a number of attacks on the "Ramushevo corridor" that formed the tenuous link between Demyansk and Staraya Russa but was unable to reduce the pocket. Things were going very badly for the Division and despite Eicke's request, for SS-TK to be withdrawn from Russia, personally to Hitler during a conference at Rastenburg on the 13th July 1942. Hitler replied that SS-TK and the surrounded Divisions would have to dig in and hold until relieved by Lieutenant General Otto von Knobelsdorff's tenth Army Corps sometime in August! Despite the nearly constant rain the Russians were preparing for a new offensive against the salient and the supply corridor and at 1.30pm July 17th the massive Russian offensive took place on all fronts of the Demjansk area, completely stunning the Germans. It was on the second day of this offensive that Max was wounded, 18th July 1942. Fortunately Max was immediately transferred to Res.Laz.Köthen and was treated here until 14.10.42. After being discharged from hospital Max had home leave from 14-10-42 until 28-10-42 then returned to the signals school at Nürnberg, arriving here on the 31-10-42.

On leave 1942....

Max served as *RV.-Truppführer* at the school until being posted to the Nachrichten School at Metz on the 25.6.1943. After nearly four months here Max was then posted to 2./SS-Nachr.Ausb u Ers Abt 2 at Unna, from the 22.10.1943 and stayed with the Abteilung until 10.7.1944. From here Max's last posting was with *SS-Nachr.Abt 501*[(2)] based at *KZ Außenlager Bunker "Fuchsbau"* at Fürstenwalde, south east of Berlin. The Bunker complex was evacuated before being overrun by the Russians in the last weeks of the war and the Abteilung did not directly engage with the enemy. It is unknown if Max was a POW, but he survived the war and settled in Herten.

Notes

[(1)] This unit was raised as *SS-Totenkopf-Nachrichten-Ersatz-Abteilung* in Nürnberg, Frankenstraße 100, at the end of 1939, to provide training for recruits for the Nachrichten-units of the *Totenkopf-Division*. With effect from March 15th 1941 its name changed to "*SS-Nachrichten-Ersatz-Abteilung*" and from October 15th 1942, it was renamed again and enlarged to "*SS-Nachrichten-Ersatz-Regiment*". The staff of the regiment were disbanded nearly one year later and the different battalions formed the independent battalions *SS-Nachrichten-Ausbildungs- und Ersatz-Abteilungen 1 to 4* with effect from November 15th 1943. The *SS-Nachr.Ausb.u.Ers.Abt 1* stayed in Nürnberg, with parts in Eichstätt and other places, until April 1945.

[(2)] *SS-Nachrichten Abteilung 501* was set up in March 1944 and changed its name to *SS-Führungs-Nachrichten-Regiment 500* in February 1945. Its main task was to act as a communications link from SS main office to its subordinate offices. The Regiment stayed mainly south east of Berlin and maintained radio links between the *SS-FHA* and various the various alarm and anti-tank units that had been established to protect the *SS-FHA*.

The Italian SS Legion
by Massimiliano Afiero

The liberation of Mussolini from Gran Sasso, September 1943.

The Waffen Miliz

Right after he was freed from imprisonment on Gran Sasso (12 September 1943), Duce Benito Mussolini explicitly asked Hitler to form two divisions of Militia, to be under *Waffen SS* leadership, that were to be engaged in the struggle against the Allied forces on the Italian front. In them elements from Fascist Militia units and from army units that had distinguished themselves on the front during previous campaigns would be combined. Italian volunteers would wear the SS uniform with the insigna with fasces. On the basis of Mussolini's requests, starting as early as the middle of September, *Reichsführer* Heinrich Himmler ordered that all Italian soldiers eager to continue to fight on the side of Germany, either from the army or from the Militia, be gathered together in a single camp. On 24 September 1943, Himmler officially announced the birth of the Italian SS legion (*Italienische Waffenverbände der SS*), as a "*Bestandteil*" unit (affiliated) to the *Waffen SS*.

Italian volunteers after 8 September 1943 (*Signal*).

Its main function was to be that of overseeing the formation and training of the new Italian military formations, on the model of foreign Legions. On 2 October 1943, Himmler emitted a special order for the training of the units of Militia, in which Mussolini's requests were partly granted. It was decided, however to form several battalions, to be used immediately in the fight against partisan brigades in northern Italy. After gaining experience and having destroyed the threat of the rebels, these battalions would then be transferred back to training camps to form the first regiments and later, after experience on the Italian front, the first Italian division was formed to be committed against the Allied forces. A second division was formed the following year. Furthermore

Himmler established that the volunteers of Militia would continue to wear the Italian uniform, but with the shoulder tabs and ranks of the SS, using insignia with a red background, instead of the usual black. These first Italian detachments were given the name of *Waffen Miliz* (Armed Militia), the combat unit of the Italian SS Legion. As the Headquarters for the grouping of volunteers the training camp of Münsingen in Württemberg, forty kilometres to the south of Stuttgart, was chosen. Simultaneously a massive propaganda campaign was started to promote the enrollment of the highest number of volunteers possible. Bear in mind that in the same period some enlistments for the birth of a new army for the Repubblica Sociale Italiana were taking place. On 9 October 1943 at the Münsingen camp 13.362 men were already present and would shortly after rise to about 15.000.

SS-Brigdf. Peter Hansen.

Italian soldiers at Münsingen (*Corbatti e Nava Collection*).

SS-Standartenführer Gustav Lombard.

As for all German units in formation, an *SS-Ausbildungsstab* (a training unit) was created, placed under the command of *SS-Brigadeführer* Peter Hansen. Unable to take the position because he was convalescing, the Italian unit was led temporarily by *SS-Standartenführer* Lombard, from the SS *Florian Geyer* cavalry division. *SS-Obersturmbannführer* Johann Eugen Corrodi von Elfenau, one of the first Swiss volunteers of the *Waffen SS*, also from the *Florian Geyer*, was appointed as chief of staff of the *Waffen Miliz*. An Italian liaison staff (*Verbindungsstab*) was formed, comprising Italian officials, placed under the command of the Lieutenant Colonel De Paolis, with the duty to assist and coordinate the work of the *SS-Ausbildungsstab*. The combat unit of the SS Italian Legion, which included Italian volunteers already present at Münsingen was further strengthened with volunteer groups from Praga, Debica and from Greece. These groups weren't redirected to Münsingen but were instead repatriated immediately after training.

Soldiers of *Prinz Eugen* Division, check vehicles and equipment abandoned by Italians after 8 September 1943.

Italian soldiers in Yugoslavia, having laid down their arms, waiting to be taken away, September 1943.

The Miliz Regiment De Maria

Among the first Italian troops to be integrated to complete the *Waffen Miliz* was the *Miliz Regiment De Maria*, under the command of the Militia Consul Paolo de Maria. Prior to 8 September, the Consul was in Split, the head of the 89th Etruscan Blackshirts Legion: the unit included about 1,500 men distributed in 89th Blackshirts Battalion of Volterra, in the 97th Blackshirts Battalion of Siena and in a machine-gun company. The 97th Battalion was under the command of the Primo Seniore della Milizia Carlo Federigo degli Oddi, the future commander of the Italian units of the *Waffen SS* on the Anzio-Nettuno front. On the 8th of September, the Legion units were in the area of Drnis, along the Dalmatian coast, tactically attached to the *Bergamo* Infantry Division. On September 9, the *Bergamo* headquarters issued the order to fall back on Sibenik and resist any attack by the Germans. In that area there were units of the SS *Prinz Eugen* Division and 114.*Jäger-Division*. After discussing the situation with his men, the entire Legion went to the side of the Germans: on that same day, De Maria met General Stahl, commander of 114.*Jäger-Division* to discuss the conditions of the transfer of his unit to the German armed forces. De Maria asked and obtained assurance that his unit was not to be used against other Italian troops and the promise that his men would be armed and refitted properly in order to continue the fight against the enemy. The German commander agreed and so the Legion was incorporated into the 114.*Jäger-Division*. Following the example of the militiamen, other groups of soldiers of *Bergamo* and other Italian units in the area, also made the same choice, voluntarily deciding to continue the war on the side of the Germans. About three thousand

The Axis Forces

Italians were thereby placed in a *Polizei-Freiwilligen-Verbände* (Police Volunteer Troop) of the German *Ordnungspolizei*, under the command of Colonel (*Oberst*) De Maria. The men continued to wear their old uniforms, with a white band on the left sleeve of the jacket with the words "*Ordnungspolizei*". Along with the German units, the unit was immediately engaged as a security force against the partisan groups. On September 27, the units of *Miliz Regiment De Maria* were ordered to leave the area of Drnis, and to move in the direction of Knin, still in the hands of the Italian units. The Italian garrison joined the Regiment.

Balkan front, September 1943, Italian soldiers "negotiating" their surrender to their German ex-allies.

Oberst **De Maria, left, while discussing with other Italian officers at Münsingen camp, Autumn 1943** (*Corbatti e Nava*).

From Knin, units moved by truck to Bihac and from Bihac, by train to Belgrade. From the capital of Serbia, again by train, following a series of erroneous orders along the march, the Italian troops went first to Austria and then to Berlin, where they arrived on October 5th. Due to the great confusion of the moment and especially the anti-Italian climate that was prevalent in the Germanic areas after the turnaround by Badoglio, members of the Regiment were transferred to a prison camp. The disappointment was great among the men, and when on 12 October they were again asked if any of them wanted to continue the fight alongside the Germans, many refused the offer: there were more than a thousand defections. On 15 October, the *Miliz Regiment De Maria*, left with two thousand men, was moved to Münsingen, where it arrived two days later. Due to the overcrowding of the camp, of De Maria's militiamen were accommodated at the nearby camp of Gensewak. When in November 1943, the Regiment returned to Italy, officially it became the 1st Regiment of Milizia Armata, based in Milan, again under the command of *Waffen-Standartenführer* De Maria. The First Battalion was under the command of *Waffen-Obersturmbannführer* Federigo degli Oddi, the Second of the *Waffen-Ostubaf.* Vittorio Gori and the Third of the *Waffen-Ostubaf.* Giorleo.

The Battaglione *Fedelissimo*

Another unit of the militia that chose in its entirety to join the *Waffen Miliz* was the XIX Battalion *Fedelissimo* stationed in the Balkans and mainly made up of volunteers from Lombardy. In early September, the Battalion was deployed in the area of Preveza, along the Ionian coast of Greece, integrated in the *Acqui* Infantry Division. The commander, the Primo Seniore della Milizia, Gilberto Fabris, on the day of the armistice, gathered his men to announce his will to continue the fight alongside the Germans. The Battalion followed him unanimously. In the area was the *1.Gebirgs-Division* under General Stettner, who was immediately contacted by Fabris to discuss the fate of his unit. The Battalion, renamed as the *Bataillon Fabris*, was assigned to *98.GebirgsJäger Regiment* and engaged along the coast as a security force against the partisan bands and in the defense of the coastline. The unit remained assigned to the German mountain division until early November, when it began the transfer to Italy in the *Waffen Miliz*, which was completed only on 1 December. Grouped in Aosta, the unit became the XI Battalion of the *Waffen Miliz*.

The SS-Bataillon Debica

At the training camp in Debica near Krakow, in the then General Government of Poland, the most combat capable battalion of the *Waffen Miliz* was formed, which was designated using the name of the Polish town. The history of this unit began in October 1943, in the camp of Feldstetten, twenty kilometers north-east of Münsingen. There, a group of interned Italian prisoners accepted the proposal by *Major* Guido Fortunato (former commander of the XIX Battalion of the 6th Bersaglieri with the CSIR) to set up a special unit of the Italian SS. Fortunato, one of the first Italian officers to throw in his lot with the Germans, had been authorized to move to the various camps to look for volunteers. Out of 400 soldiers who responded to his call, only 38 were considered suitable and transferred to Münsingen for initial training. In early December, Fortunato with the core of Feldstetten volunteers, reinforced by several hundred other volunteers (20 officers and 571 men), were transferred to *SS-Truppen-Übungsplatz Heidelager*, east of Debica: it was a special school for the German SS, where they were training the reconnaissance groups in support of the divisions, and where many foreign units were also being trained. The volunteer training was

Federigo degli Oddi in 1944.

Waffen-Stubaf. Fortunato.

SS soldiers at Debica, 1943.

much harder and intense than that given in Münsingen, which transformed the Italian volunteers into true *Waffen SS* combatants. For this reason, the unit was called from the beginning "*SS-Bataillon Debica*" (the official name was *Italienische Freiwilligen SS-Bataillon*), while all other units of the *Waffen Miliz* could not use the term SS. The volunteers wore German uniforms and wore black collar badges.

Training with an *MG-34* at *SS-Truppen-Übungsplatz Heidelager* (*Reimo Leol Collection*).

Organization of units

Vittorio Mussolini visits the Italian soldiers in training in Germany (*Collezione Privata Saronno*).

The Italian volunteers in Münsingen were organized into twelve battalions. The first three, formed the 1st Regiment of Milizia Armata, born from the transformation of *Miliz Regiment De Maria*. Due to the high number of available officers, a battalion of officers was also formed. The personnel considered unfit for combat were grouped in a work battalion. A supervisory unit consisting of ex-Carabinieri was also formed for safety in the camp. As for the equipment and the supply of weapons, the Italian volunteers continued to wear their old uniforms. The German High Command distributed a metal skull insignia to all the volunteers, to be applied on the lapel of the jacket or cap, as a unique symbol of official identification of the *Waffen Miliz* members.

The Axis Forces

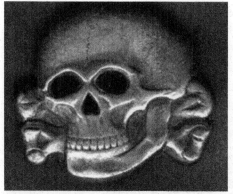

Metal skull insignia.

On 11 November 1943, the Italian volunteers swore the oath of loyalty to Adolf Hitler:

*Davanti a Dio presto questo sacro giuramento:
che nella lotta per la mia patria italiana
contro i suoi nemici sarò in maniera assoluta
obbediente ad Adolf Hitler,
supremo comandante dell'esercito tedesco,
e quale soldato valoroso sarò pronto in ogni momento
a dare la mia vita per questo giuramento*

(*Before God I make this sacred oath: that in the struggle for my Italian homeland against its enemies will be in an absolute obedience to Adolf Hitler, the supreme commander of the German army, and as a brave soldier will be ready at all times to give my life for this oath*).

SS-Hstuf. **Thaler** and *Waffen-Stubaf.* **Fortunato**.

Following the ceremony the volunteers were informed of their imminent return to Italy. At the same time they were offered the opportunity to be transferred into the armed forces of the Italian Social Republic or to other formations of the *Waffen SS*. And so, a thousand volunteers chose to go in RSI units while only a hundred chose to be transferred to other units of the *Waffen SS*. There were also some defections: about 500 volunteers preferred to return to prison camps after the circulation of false news of a possible transfer of Italian troops to the Eastern Front. Before returning to Italy, some personnel of the *Waffen Miliz*, several hundred men, were sent to specialized schools at Dachau, Weimar, Dresden and Szczecin (Stettin).

Bibliography
S.Corbatti, M.Nava, "*Sentire-Pensare-Volere: storia della Legione SS italiana*", Ritter Edizioni
AA.VV. "*Italiani nella Waffen SS, numero speciale Ritterkreuz I/2009*", Associazione Culturale Ritterkreuz

FOREIGN VOLUNTEER LEGION MILITARY AWARD & INSIGNIA
by Rene Chavez

Vidkun Quisling and Norwegian Volunteers, 1942.

Volunteers of the *Légion des Voluntaires Français*, 1941.

I'm writing this article relating to a very important WWII military history subject about foreign volunteers that joined the German *Wehrmacht* and were allowed to wear by the Germans, military decorations that were provided by their own collaborationist political parties that existed during German occupation. This article provides a brief history relating to Western Europeans that joined the German army and I will illustrate by country the military insignia and some of the important military decorations that were awarded to these volunteers. When Operation *Barbarossa* started already foreigners from neutral and occupied European countries were either already in a German formation such as the Spanish Blue Division or were going to German recruiting centers around occupied Europe and enlisted to join the German *Wehrmacht*. Most of the Europeans that came from Scandinavian countries (Denmark, and Norway) and Western Europe such as the Netherlands and Flanders (Dutch speaking Belgium) ended up being recruited by the *Waffen-SS* and formed their own formations referred by the Germans as Legions. Meanwhile Europeans from France and Wallonie (French speaking Belgium) were being recruited by the German Army to form their own Legions. Neutral Spain ended up forming a whole German designated infantry division. These Legions formation were popular with the collaborationist pro-Nazi parties that supported them during German occupation.

Norway

Norwegian volunteers with the flag of *Den Norske Legion*.

Above is a locally made Norwegian National Flag sleeve patch worn on the SS uniforms by legion volunteers.

Norway was occupied by the Germans as early as April 1940 during the German invasion. Norway already had a pro-Nazi political party called the *Nasjonal Samling* ("National Gathering") that was formed in 1933 and was under the leadership of Vidkun Quisling. Quisling wanted to persuade Hitler that the Norwegian government would support the German occupation. Hitler remained unreceptive to the idea. Hence, on the first day of invasion, Quisling burst into the NRK studios in Oslo and made a nationwide broadcast declaring himself prime minister and ordering all resistance halted at once. This did not please the Germans who wanted the legitimate government to remain in place. Nevertheless, when it became obvious that the Norwegian parliament would not surrender, the Germans quickly came to recognize Quisling. They demanded that the Royal legitimate King Haakon formally appoint him as prime minister and return his government to Oslo; in effect, giving legal sanction to the invasion. However Quisling was removed in favor of a German administration led by *Reichskommissar* Josef Terboven who took over power by forming his own cabinet. Quisling was consequently re-instituted as head of state on 20 February 1942, although Terboven still had all the power. Under Quisling pro-Nazi party and German support represented by *Reichskommissar* Terboven united to create a Norwegian volunteer legion. A massive recruiting rally was held on the University Square in Oslo on 4 July 1941. The Legion was sent to Bjolsen Skole camp in Norway where uniforms were received. The Legionnaires were surprised to receive German SS uniforms since they had expected to wear Norwegian or Finnish uniforms. On 29 July 1941, the first 300 Norwegian volunteers arrived in Kiel, Germany, and were sent to Fallingbostel Training Camp. By August 1941 the total number of recruits had grown to over 700. By the end of 1941, it had the strength of 1218 men, with an additional reserve battalion provided for replacement. The officers were sent to Lauenburg training camp. The Legion was officially named *"Den Norske Legion"* (The Norwegian Legion). In December 1941, after completing six months enlistment, Legionnaires re-enlisted for another six months. Originally the plan was to have them serve in the Finnish sector of the Eastern Front but because of the critical situations elsewhere in Russia, the Legion was sent by train to the Leningrad Front. This Legion had no contacts with their compatriots in the *Wiking* Division who were considered full *Waffen-SS* cadre personnel.

The Hird Arm-Shield: Members of the *"Nasjonal Samling"* and its paramilitary arm *"Hird"* were allowed to wear their emblem, a circular St Olaf's Cross with upright swords in silver and black as a sleeve patch.

Den Norske Legion Collar Tab: Above is a locally made Norwegian Legion collar patch (right collar only) displaying a Norwegian lion holding an axe tied to a black wool collar tab.

Arthur Quist, Kdr of DNL.

By the end of December, the Legion's strength dropped to 20 officers and 678 other ranks. On 1 March 1943, the Legion including the 1st Police Company, was withdrawn from the Front lines and sent to Norway on home leave. In May 1943, about 600 veterans were sent to the Grafenwöhr training camp in Germany where the *III.SS-Pz.Korps* was being formed. The Legion was disbanded and the Norwegian volunteers were offered to re-enlist in the new *SS-Pz.Gr.Rgt.24 'Norge'*. Norwegians that fought in the Eastern Front were awarded German combat decorations, however, in spite of the strict German regulations, many volunteers were tolerated by the Germans and allowed to wear their political party military awards.

The Axis Forces

Frontkjemper

One of the most recognizable awards was the *"Frontkjemper"* Front Fighter award shown. This badge was instituted in October 1943 by Vidkun Quisling and awarded for bravery to Norwegian volunteers and German cadre who saw action on the Eastern Front. This badge was made by the Norwegian firm in Oslo *"Holmsen"* and was issued in one class only, silver. The badge shows a Nordic warrior holding a shield and drawn sword, and is standing in an archway, which bore the letters "FRONT KJEMPER" (Front Fighter) in pseudo runic script.

The "Brave and Faithful" Order

Another interesting award was the so-called "Brave and Faithful" Order. The cross with crossed swords was awarded to Norwegian members of Quisling's political party "Hird." The award was given for merit and bravery and was only issued once but immediately was removed Hitler forbid it to be worn on German uniforms.

Above are two crosses. The first one being produced in 1942/43, which shows the date "1941" marked in the center of the cross. The reverse is marked with the inscription "TAPPER OG TRO" (Brave and Loyal). The cross is missing its ribbon, which has two red stripes on each edge and a yellow gold color stripe in the center. Later in 1944 the date was removed or covered up by adding in the center the Hird emblem an eagle clutching the sun cross. The cross has the ribbon, which was also attached to the earlier "1941" cross.

Flag of the *Frikorp Danmark*, 1941.

Denmark

On April 1940, the Germans invaded Denmark with virtually no resistance encountered by the defending Danes. With the events taking place during Operation Barbarossa, the Germans started a recruitment of Danish and Norwegian volunteers for the *Nordland* Regiment. This regiment was sent to the eastern front in June 1941 and remained there until March 1943. Meanwhile, a separate inclusive Danish volunteer formation was in the plans by the Germans with the approval of the Danish Government. The legion was officially authorized and announced by the Danish government on 28 June 1941. This formation was open to men who were currently in the Danish armed forces or who had completed their conscript service within a period of ten years. Unlike other western European volunteers, the Danish King and government granted equal veteran rights for all volunteers. Those who were career soldiers were promised the retention of their own military rank status. A Danish Press release to allow Danish men in joining the new formation was posted on 8 July 1941. Immediately recruiting offices were placed all over Denmark with the main office located in Copenhagen, on *Rosenvaengets Alle 32*. Initial drafts of 430 Danish soldiers were incorporated into an SS battalion under the command of former Danish Army Colonel Christian Peder Kryssing.

From left, von Schalburg and Kryssing.

Per Sörensen with Trifos Collar Tab.

The *Dannebrog* Collar Tab.

These volunteers were sent for training at Hamburg on 20 July 1941. In early August, a second group from recruited Danish volunteers including 200 Danes transferring from the *Nordwest* Regiment was formed at the Hamburg training facilities. The new formation designated as the "*SS-Freiwilligen Verband Danemark*". In Denmark, it was commonly referred as the "*Freikorps Danmark*," thus evoking the memory of a Danish expeditionary force, which fought in the White Army against the Bolsheviks during the post-1917 Russian Civil War. Upon reaching the training grounds in Hamburg, a special three legged *"Trifos"* collar tabs were issued. This was also the emblem of the *Nordwest* Regiment. In addition, *"Freikorps Danmark"* Cuff Band were issued and worn by the volunteers. Interestingly a *"Dannebrog"* (Danish flag) collar tab was also issued and worn by the volunteers of the Replacement Company for a very short time until April 1943. On 11 June 1943, the SS *Nordland* Regiment and the Freikorps veterans were merged as the *SS-Panzer-Grenadier Regiment 24 'Danmark'*.

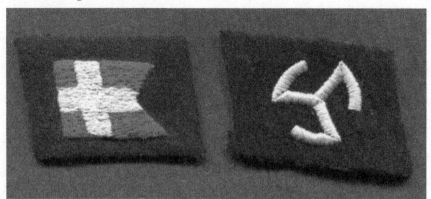

Illustrated is a very rare locally made Danish flag and German made Trifos collar tab.

The Schalburg Corps

The Schalburg Corps was the branch of the Germanic SS, named after Christian von Schalburg, former commander of the *Freikorps Danmark* who was KIA. The Danish Germanic SS was formed on February 2, 1943. By March 30, 1943 it was renamed *"Schalburg Korps"*. Most of the members were fomer veterans of the *Freikorps Danmark*. Members who had no combat experience had to go to through a six week political indoctrination and combat training.

The Schalburg Cross

Was a military Germanic SS decoration that was awarded to Schalburg members for recognition of service against the Danish Resistance and for those serving or killed in action in the Eastern Front. It has been recorded once that a cross was awarded to a *Schalburg Corps* member KIA. This cross was instituted later then 1943, otherwise pictures would have surfaced of it being worn. There were two classes issued one for officers and NCOs and the other for enlisted. Both crosses were die struck and measured 50 mm x 50 mm. Enlisted men wore a cream white color painted cross with golden outer edges. The cross has a center medallion with the outer ring inscription *"TROSKAB VOR AERE"* (LOYALTY OUR HONOR) and golden oak leaves and the center ring showing a white mobile swastika with a opaque red color in the background. The officers cross was the same design but the color was enameled. The reverse on both crosses is flat with semi scoop shape in the center and a single short pin attached to the top of the cross.

The Netherlands

The Netherlands is an enclave culturally and politically of their German neighbors. On 10 May 1940, Holland was occupied by Germany. The Germans drove the Queen with her cabinet into exile. The Dutch were then governed under the Commission of Arthur Seyss-Inquart. The German occupation forces established recruiting centers in all the major cities of Holland. Many Dutch men volunteered to join the German *Wehrmacht*. The majority however enlisted in *Waffen-SS* units. These men were members of pro-Nazi Parties such as the Dutch National Socialist Movement "N.S.B" led by Anton Mussert. In May 1941, a contingent of 631 Dutch men with a cadre of German personnel was incorporated into the SS-Regiment *Westland* and attached to the SS-Division *Wiking*. Prior to the outbreak of the German-Russian war, a large contingent of Dutch men had enlisted in the *6.SS-Nordwest*. It was decided to form a Dutch formation within the lines of the *Nordwest* Regiment. On 16 July 1941, a Dutch Legion Battalion was created. A contingent of 2000 volunteers wearing civilian clothing and Dutch uniforms departed to the SS training camp at Debica in Poland. By August 1941, two battalions of Dutch volunteers were formed. These two battalions were placed under the leadership of a 69year old former Dutch Army Chief of Staff Lt-General H. A. Seyffardt. In September 1941, the Legion was sent for further training at Ayrs in East Prussia, where it was joined by a third battalion formed from Dutch Nazi Storm Troopers. A special "Wolf Hook" Pennant emblem was presented to the newly formed Legion. In late September, with the dissolution of the SS "*Nordwest*" Regiment, the "*Freiwilligen Legion Nierderlande*" (Dutch Volunteer Legion), became a fully independent entity. After advanced training at Ayrs, a contingent of 2600 troops departed to Danzig from which it traveled by sea to Libau, Latvia, accompanied by its own all-Dutch Red Cross and its own propaganda company of some 50 reporters and press cameramen. In early 1942, the Dutch Legion

A group of Dutch Volunteers with Wolf Hook Collar Tab.

These volunteers wore German SS uniforms. A Dutch national sleeve shield was worn on their uniform and a cuff title bearing the Legion's name.

The Axis Forces

moved by foot and later by motorized transportation to the Volkhov Front, in the vicinity of Gusi-Gova north of Lake Ilmen near Leningrad (today Saint Petersburg).

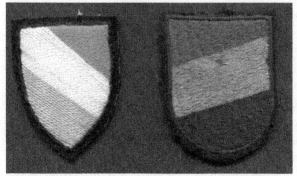

The Dutch shield on the left side was locally made in the Netherlands while the shield on the right is German made.

A standard SS type collar tab (right collar only) displaying a *"Wolf Hook"* was issued and worn.

The Mussert Cross (*Rene Chavez Collection*).

The Mussert Cross

The Dutch NSB party leader Anton Mussert produced and issued many military decorations that were presented to Legion volunteers and Party members. One of the most recognizable is the so-called Mussert Cross. This decoration was issued for bravery and merit to NSB members in German service. The cross illustrated is made of three parts from enamel and high quality gilt finished metal. The outside edge of the cross is in black enamel on both sides with inner portion finished in translucent red. A separate white medallion is soldered to the front and back of the cross. The front side shows gilt wolf hook over swastika with oak leaves. The back side shows around the top edge a ring the motto of the NSB in gilt *"Hou En Trou"* and oak leaves on the bottom edge. The center of the disc has the name "MUSSERT and the date 1941." The ribbon shows the Dutch national colors. The award came in a two piece maroon outer card case. The award was probably worn however it was not authorized to be worn on the German uniform.

Flanders

A *Waffen-SS* volunteer of the Regiment *'Westland'*.

The *Flemish Legion* parading through Bruxelles, 1941.

Belgium is a divided country, with two different social classes. One class, Flemish, is racially and linguistically Germanic. The other class, *Wallonien*, is French speaking and racially mixed Celtic and Roman origin. Both are united by their strong Catholic faith. The Flemings, like the Wallonies, had their own pro-Nazi parties. In May 1940, the Lowlands were invaded by the Germans and immediately recruiting centers were set up in the occupied countries. The response was favourable and two SS regiments *"Westland"* and *"Nordland"* were created. These regiments contained Germanic volunteers but with 50% German composition. The *"Westland"* and *"Nordland"* Regiments were incorporated into the SS *"Wiking"* Division. The first regiment composed in its entirely of Dutch, Danish and Flemish personnel was designated as the *"6.SS Nordwest Regiment."* This 600 man regiment was formed in June 1941, and comprised of three companies. The members of the *Nordwest* Regiment were still in training at Hamburg-Langehorn, when Germany invaded Russia. There was a widespread desire among the volunteers to participate actively in the campaign, especially those men who were members of pro-Nazi Parties and wanted their political affiliation represented in the Eastern Front. Shortly afterwards a Flemish Legion was announced and immediately Flemish personnel from the *Nordwest* Regiment were transfer into the new Legion. It was deemed necessary for the legion to receive proper SS combat training. On July 14, the three Flemish companies were shipped to the east by rail to Poland. While in Radom training camp, the Flemish formation was upgraded to the SS Infantry Battalion *"Flandern."* The 1st, 6th and 8th companies from the *Nordwest* were converted to the 1st, 2nd and 3rd companies of the

Legion. In early August, a draft of 405 young Flemings enlisted into the Legion along with the other volunteers who were quartered at Grafenwöhr, Bavaria. These troops were used to form a fourth unit. By the end of August, there were 875 Flemings in the Legion not taking into account the 696 Flemings already in service with the *"Wiking"* Division. Flemish personnel wore *Waffen-SS* uniforms. The Flemish wore a German made arm-shield on their left sleeve showing the national crest, a black lion on a gold field. A cuff title bearing the words *"Legioen Vlaanderen"* was issued and worn on their lower left sleeve.

Flemish Volunteer Legion Arm-Shield.

A Flemish *Rottenführer* on the Eastern Front.

A three legged sun-wheel insignia was worn on the right collar-patch.

The battalion *"Flandern"* received orders transferring it to the Heidelager training camp near Debica, Poland. At the Debica SS camp, the legionnaires were soon joined by the rest of the Flemish personnel. The Flemish Legion was joined with the Dutch Legion for combat training. On early September, the Flemish Battalion left for the SS Camp at Arys in East Prussia. On 24 September, the SS headquarters in Berlin officially bestowed the title *"SS Freiwilligen Legion Flandern."* The Flemish Legion mostly fought northern front of Leningrad.

It was eventually withdrawn from the battlefront in May 1943 and sent to the training camp at Bohemia, where it was disbanded and remnants of the Legion had the choice to volunteer for the new SS Brigade (*6.SS-Freiwilligen-Sturmbrigade 'Langemarck'*).

The Tollenaere Honor Badge

The Tollenaere Honor badge was the second most prestigious award and was rendered in two classes, silver and bronze, although there is no evidence shown that the silver class was ever worn. The badge honors the death of the VNV Black Brigade Leader Dr. Reimond Tollenaere who was killed in action at Kopzy, near Leningrad on 22 January 1942. The badge shows the Dutch wolf's hook, a small rectangular box with the motto "TROUW" (Loyalty) and a sword in the background crossing it. The bottom part is a circular ring with the Flemish motto "AANR TOLLENAERE KOPZY JAN 1942" indicating the date and place where he was killed. This badge was awarded for loyalty and sacrifice.

The Tollenaere Honor Badge.

Reimond Tollenaere.

Swearing-in ceremony for Walloons volunteers.

Wallonie

Fascist political parties already existed in Belgium by the time Germany began occupying the country. These political parties were already prepared to collaborate with the Germans. Leon Degrelle was a pro-Nazi collaborator who founded the "Rexist Party." The Rexist party was composed of Walloons who wanted a separate sovereignty. When Germany invaded Belgium, Leon Degrelle was on placed under arrest by the government for fear he would collaborate with the Germans. German troops, discovered him in a French prison and he was promptly released. As soon as the war with Russia broke out Leon Degrelle and his followers joined the *Wehrmacht*. They were known as the "Corps Franc Wallonie" (Free Corps Wallonie). In August 1941, the Corps was sent to Poland for basic training.

Wallonie Volunteer Legion Arm-Shield.

Leon Degrelle in German uniform.

The Walloons were provided with army uniforms. A German made arm shield showing the Belgium national colors was worn on their uniforms. This Legion of 1500 men was registered as the "373.Infanterie Bataillon." By June 1943, 1600 veterans of the Legion were incorporated into the *Waffen-SS* (*5.SS-Sturmbrigade 'Wallonien'*).

The Wallonie Rexist Honor Badge

The Walloon Rexist badge also known as the Blood Order was instituted in 1941. The badge can be found in three classes: bronze, silver and gold. The bronze and silver badge shows the Walloon Bergundy cross with a sword crossing it surrounded by a circular ring with the French inscription that reads "Bravoure Honneur Fidelite" (Bravery, Honor and Loyalty).

The reverse of the badge is somewhat different between the bronze and silver class. Both have hollow backs but the silver badge has a thin Belgium style pin with hinge and a broad "C" style catch with no serial number. The bronze on the other hand can be found in two styles.

Sturmmann of *Wallonien* with Rexist Honor Badge.

Interestingly the early issue bronze badges did not have the pin assembly instead it had in the reverse three loops soldered directly to the metal. These loops were secured in the uniform by thread. The bronze badges do not have a maker's mark but all have serial numbers. Later on a second group of bronze badges were produced but with the same reverse as the silver and all have serial numbers. Not much is known on the gold Rexist badges, only that two have been known to be issued, one to Leon Degrelle and another to a Walloon chaplain. Also there was a gold Rexist badge with diamonds that was issued to Victor Matthys who took leadership of the Rexist movement while Degrelle was in combat in the Eastern Front. In addition, another very rare Rexist badge was produced and issued to Flemings that settled in the French speaking part of Belgium and represented the VNV political party in Wallonia. These badges have the same inscription but written in Dutch "MOED, EER & TROUW." In November 1944, RFSS Himmler authorized the award to be worn on the German uniform when the Walloon Army formation was transferred to the *Waffen-SS*.

France

When Germany invaded Russia in June 1941 it caused great excitement among the collaborating political parties and para-military home based formations. They now found a new unity in their desire to participate in the Russian campaign. The first recruiting center was opened at the recruiting center located in "12 rue Auber, Paris," additional recruiting centers was also placed all over France. On 18 July 1941, the "Légion des Voluntaires Français contre le Bolshevisme (LVF)" was established. Initially the Vichy Government had enacted a law that forbade Frenchmen from enlisting into "foreign armies" to prevent them from joining with the Free French forces of exiled General Charles de Gaulle. Since the LVF was a private affair, Marshal Petain amended the law so that no objection would be raised for Frenchmen enlisting into the LVF. These volunteers were placed in the Borgnis-Desbordes barracks at Versailles. A total of 5800 Frenchmen were selected into the LVF. They wore standard German army uniforms and had the French national arm shield inscribed "FRANCE" placed on their right sleeve. A Colonel Roger Labonne assumed command of the legion. On 4 September, the first draft of volunteers of 828 officers and men left to the "*Truppenuebungsplatz Debica*" (troop exercise area Debica), located in Poland. On 20 September, the second Legion contingent of 896 men was sent to Debica troop training barracks. By October 1941, the LVF was up to a strength of two battalions with 181 officers and 2271 other ranks with a liaison staff of 35 Germans. The LVF was registered as "*638.Infanterie Regiment*" (638th Infantry Regiment) of the German Army. By the end of October, both battalions proceeded by rail to

French Volunteers on Eastern Front, December 1941.

A French Volunteer with arm shield 'France', 1941.

Smolensk and then by truck and on foot towards the front line near Moscow. In July 1943, a separate formation composed of French volunteers joined the *Waffen-SS*.

French Volunteer Legion Arm-Shield.

A French Volunteer, december 1941.

La Croix de Guerre Légionnaire

The Croix de Guerre Legionnaire was a decoration originally intended to be awarded to members of the *"Légion Tricolore"* (Tricolor Legion). But because of the short lived formation of the *Légion Tricolore* (officially created on 28 June 1942 and dissolved on 28 December 1942) and the fact that members of the legion never actually fought combat in the Eastern Front, the award was for all intents and purposes given to LVF veterans, as well as to soldiers of the short lived *"Phalange Africaine"* (African phalanx). The LVF cross was created on July 6, 1942. On 16 September 1942, it was officially recognized by the Vichy government. The LVF cross was formed from parts of the overall 1939 Croix de Guerre model and has a standard width of 38mm. The swords were removed, side metal traces were the sword were removed are normally visible. The swords were substituted by a stylized laurel wreath 25mm outer diameter.

The Axis Forces

Retro of the Cross.

Spanish volunteer, 1941.

Each side of the wreath is made of 12 leaves and is tied by a large ribbon knot. The laurel wreath is die-stamped and is welded to the four arms of the cross around the center. The laurel wreath is obviously a reference to the Napoleonic Empire. The center medallion (circular disc) of the Croix de Guerre was replaced by another medallion of 14mm in diameter that shows the bronze emblem of the French imperial eagle holding four lightning rods in its talons and the French Tricolor shield placed in the center of the eagle's chest. The tricolor shield has the inscription "FRANCE" on top. The reverse shows the medallion with the inscription: "CROIX DE GUERRE LEGIONNAIRE." The medallion has a concave shape on both sides and the cross has a golden bronze color. The ribbon color was totally different from the official 1939 French sanction ribbons but similar in color to the Vichy Cross ribbons. The LVF cross is held by a green ribbon showing on each side a wide vertical black edges with seven vertical black stripes. Supposedly about 300 LVF crosses were distributed between 1942 and 1944.

SPAIN

When the news of the German invasion of Russia reached Spain on 22 June 1941, the Spanish Foreign Minister Ramon Serrano Suñer offered the German Ambassador Eberhard von Stohrer military assistance from the "Falange" (Spanish Fascist Party) and the Army. This offer was provided in return for Germany's military contribution and of Russia's involvement in the Spanish civil war. The General Staff issued a directive on 28 June 1941, to the commanders of the various military regions in Spain and Spanish Morocco, which laid down the terms for recruitment. The volunteers were used to form the *"Division Española de Voluntarios"* (Spanish Division of Volunteers). The volunteers were to be enlisted for the duration of the campaign. All officers above the rank of second lieutenant were to be army regulars. The division was structured according to the traditional Spanish model with four infantry regiments, each bearing the name of their commanding officer. However since the German infantry division had only three regiments, the Spaniards had to reorganize and place the excess personnel on reserve. Each regiment was composed of units from different military regions. In early July, a Spanish Military Commission was sent to the Reserve Headquarters in Berlin to discuss the structure and organization of the German Division. The Spaniards advised the Germans that they were recruiting a division of 640 officers, 2272 NCOs and 15,780 troops. The Spaniards discovered that the Germans required at least 580 NCOs more and about 100 fewer officers. In addition the Germans demanded their own transportation of 300 trucks and 400 motorcycles. On July 7, after much negotiating between the Spanish Commission and both the German and Spanish Embassies, the commander-in-chief of the reserve army, General Fritz Fromm informed the Spaniards that the Reich would bear all costs of the Spanish Division. The troops would receive combat pay, dependents allowance, hospitalization and free franking privileges. The logistic support required to support the Blue Division was provided by the German *Wehrmacht*. By August 21, 18,000 troops 5610 horses and 765 vehicles were assembled and loaded into freight cars to a camp at Grafenwöhr in Bavaria under the leadership of General Agustin Muñoz Grandes.

General Agustin Muñoz Grandes.

Spanish Volunteers at Poselok, 1942.

Spanish Volunteer Legion Arm-Shield.

These troops were immediately outfitted in German uniforms (with the German made Spanish national arm shield inscribed "ESPAÑA" placed on their right shoulder). It was officially named the 250th Infantry Division but commonly known as the Spanish Blue Division. The division was broken up into three regiments the remainder of personnel was distributed among the regiments. This division was composed of Army and Falangist personnel who were accustomed to wearing blue shirts. By October 1941, the division was assigned to Ist Corps, which was deployed along the front line between Novgorod and Lake Ilmen. The divisional staff had its headquarters at Grigorovo, thereafter it was based in the outskirts of Leningrad.

By August 1943, the Blue Division withdrew from the front line prior to repatriation of the bulk of the troops. On October 17, the Blue Division withdrew from the Leningrad front to a reserve position behind Oranienbaum. The return of veterans to Spain was done with a minimum of ceremony and by November 163,347 men they were quietly repatriated.

Spanish Volunteers in march, december 1941.

Spanish sentinel, 1942.

The Spanish Eastern Front Medal

The *"Erinnerungsmedaille fur die Spanischen Freiwilligen im Kampf gegen den Bolschewismus"* (Commemorative Medal for Spanish Volunteers in the Struggle against Bolshevism) is also referred as the Spanish Blue Division Eastern Front medal. It was instituted on 3rd January 1944, to recognize the 250th Infantry Division. The medal was die struck in zinc alloy with a bronze wash. It shows on the bottom obverse a swastika with a spray of laurel leafs emanating from each side. The leaves are arranged differently on both ends. A sword crosses the center with two shields superimposed on it. The shield on the left shows the *Wehrmacht* eagle while the other featured the Falangists crushed arrows. Directly above the shields is an M-43 German helmet facing left, with the faint outline of the *Wehrmacht* Eagle on it. The reverse bottom has an Iron Cross, with the ribbon spread above it intertwined with a spread of leaves on both sides. On the left it shows laurels while on the right oak leaves. In the center, the medal bore the inscription "DIVISION ESPAÑOLA DE VOLUNTARIOS EN

RUSSIA" (Division of Spanish Volunteers in Russia). On top of the medal, the ribbon ring normally is stamped with the number "1," which indicates that it was produced by the German firm "Deschler und Sohn."

The medal measures 32mm in diameter and 1mm in width. The ribbon is 30mm wide, in the center is a 3mm yellow stripe followed by two wide red stripes then two white stripes and two black edges. The Spanish medal above shows the German Eastern Front ribbon instead of the Spanish. The medal was presented in a maroon box with paper hinge or in an envelope in which the entire name of the award was written in gothic script. In both cases the award was wrapped in tissue paper. A German award Certificate was issued with the award.

This concludes this article relating to insignia and military awards rendered to European volunteers from western occupied European countries of Norway, Denmark, Belgium (Flanders & Wallonia), The Netherlands, and France as well as the neutral country of Spain.

Bibliography

John R. Angolia, "*Cloth insignia of the SS*", 2nd Edition, Bender Press, 1983.

John R. Angolia, "*For Führer and Fatherland, military awards of the Third Reich*", 3rd Edition, Bender Press, 1976.

John R. Angolia & Adolph Schlicht, "*Uniforms and traditions of the German Army 1933-45*", (Vol. I & II), Bender Press, 1984 & 1986.

David Littlejohn, "*Foreign Legions of The Third Reich*", (VOL. I-IV), Bender Publishing, 1979, 1981, 1985 & 1987.

W. & Deeter, R. Odegard, "*Foreign Volunteers of Hitler's Germany*", DO Enterprises.

Spanish Volunteers.

CPSIA information can be obtained
at www.ICGtesting.com
Printed in the USA
BVOW04s0836290817
493313BV00007B/6/P